CHESHIRE
AND
STAFFORDSHIRE

LEICESTERSHIRE

S T A F F O R D 'S H I R E

SHROPSHIRE

WORCESTERSHIRE

Eccleshall

Stone

Uttoxeter

Tutbury

Chartley

Gt.Haywood Abbots Bromley

Burton-on-Trent

Gnosall

STAFFORD °Tixall

Alrewas

Rugeley

Lichfield

Lepley ° Penkridge

Cannock

Tamworth

Brewood

Bushbury

Wolverhampton

Darlaston

Walsall

Bilston ° Wednesb

Himley Tipton ° West E

Dudley ° Oldbury

Brierley Hill ° Smet

Cradley °

W

E

English Miles

0 2 4 6 8 10 20

THE SHADING INDICATES LAND OF OVER 500 FEET IN HEIGHT

NORTH MIDLAND COUNTRY

The Face of Britain Series

*Uniform with this Volume in Size
and Style*

ENGLISH LAKELAND
By DOREEN WALLACE

COTSWOLD COUNTRY
By H. J. MASSINGHAM

CHILTERN COUNTRY
By H. J. MASSINGHAM

THE HOME COUNTIES
By S. P. B. MAIS

ENGLISH DOWNLAND
By H. J. MASSINGHAM

NORTH COUNTRY
By EDMUND VALE

THE HIGHLANDS OF SCOTLAND
By HUGH QUIGLEY

THE LOWLANDS OF SCOTLAND
By GEORGE SCOTT-MONCRIEFF

THE FACE OF IRELAND
By MICHAEL FLOYD

WELSH BORDER COUNTRY
By P. T. JONES

SHAKESPEARE'S COUNTRY
By JOHN RUSSELL

EAST ANGLIA
By DOREEN WALLACE

SOUTH-EASTERN SURVEY
By RICHARD WYNDHAM

BATSFORD BOOKS

1 WINDLEY, DERBYSHIRE

From the painting by
Douglas Percy Bliss

THE FACE OF BRITAIN

◆

NORTH MIDLAND COUNTRY

A SURVEY OF CHESHIRE, DERBYSHIRE
LEICESTERSHIRE, NOTTINGHAMSHIRE
AND STAFFORDSHIRE

By

J. H. INGRAM

Illustrated from Prints, Engravings and Photographs

B. T. BATSFORD LTD.
LONDON · NEW YORK
TORONTO · SYDNEY

First published, Winter 1947-8

*Made and Printed in Great Britain by the
Western Printing Services, Ltd., Bristol, for
the Publishers*
B. T. BATSFORD, LTD.
LONDON: 15 North Audley Street, W.1
and MALVERN WELLS, Worcestershire
NEW YORK: 122 East 55th Street
TORONTO: 480-6 University Avenue
SYDNEY: 156 Castlereagh Street

PREFACE

A BOOK which tells of the English countryside owes much to the labours of many other persons beside the author. Scholars and observers long dead, and men and women who still work in the fields and factories of Midland England, have all helped in the making of this book, by contributing something of their knowledge, and to them, and all those other patient investigators who preceded him along the delectable byways of local history, biography, archaeology and folk-lore, the author tenders humble thanks. As will be seen, the list is a long one, and ranges from William Webb, who was clerk to the mayors' courts of Chester in the seventeenth century and Celia Fiennes, who rode through England on a side-saddle in the reign of William and Mary, to Dr. Johnson and his Boswell, Izaak Walton, and T. A. Coward, who was writing of natural history in Cheshire within the memory of many of my readers. To the late Edwin Royce, editor of the *Northern Rambler*, the author feels especially grateful for much kindly advice, information and criticism.

Among living persons who deserve their meed of praise are the good people of Leicester, for hospitality and information, and the country folk who dwell among the high lands where Cheshire, Staffordshire and Derbyshire meet; in particular, Mr. Thomas Mullins, farmer, of Wincle in the Dane Valley. Thanks are also due to the Leicester Footpath Association, the City of Leicester Publicity and Development Department, the Housing Centre, the Publicity Officer for Chester, and the Town Clerks of Birmingham, Derby and Nottingham, for permission to quote from information supplied by their respective organisations; also to Mr. T. H. Gough and the proprietors of the *Dudley Herald* for quotations from *Black Country Stories and Customs*, and to Mr. Francis Thompson for information about Chatsworth House. The author would also like to express his indebtedness to Mr. Arnold Fellow's book *The Wayfarer's Companion* which accompanied him on various journeys made for the purpose of visiting places described herein; it proved invaluable.

Last, but not least, thanks are due to Mr. Harry Batsford and his colleagues for their assistance in the preparation of the volume and for the admirable discretion with which they corrected sundry errors and spelling mistakes.

CONTENTS

ACKNOWLEDGMENT

THE Publishers wish to express their thanks to the photographers whose work is reproduced in these pages, namely, Messrs. Aerofilms, Ltd., for Figs. 15, 54; Mr. F. L. Attenborough, M.A., for Figs. 20, 89, 97, 98; Mr. Maurice Beck, for Figs. 42, 43; Mr. W. J. B. Blake, for Fig. 45; Mr. R. R. Bull, for Fig. 28; The Central Office of Information, for Figs. 16, 80, 94, 114; Messrs. Central Press Photos, Ltd., for Fig. 4; the late Brian C. Clayton, for Figs. 7, 21, 64; Messrs. Country Life, Ltd., for Fig. 56; Mr. Fred H. Crossley, F.S.A., for Figs. 70, 74; Messrs. Dorien Leigh, Ltd., for Fig. 12; Mr. T. Edmondson, for Fig. 52; Mr. H. Felton, F.R.P.S., for Figs. 38, 67; Mr. Paul Fripp, for Fig. 36; Messrs. Fox Photos, Ltd., for Figs. 6, 81, 82; Mr. Graystone-Bird, for Fig. 99; Mr. E. M. Hickmans, for Fig. 30; Mr. A. J. Houghton, for Fig. 113; Mr. S. A. Jeavons, for Fig. 27; Messrs. H. & V. Joel, for Figs. 23, 77; Messrs. The Keystone View Co., Ltd., for Fig. 39; Mr. W. North, for Figs. 109, 110; Mr. Staniland Pugh, for Fig. 84; Mr. Raymond Richards, F.S.A., for Figs. 63, 69, 73, from *Old Cheshire Churches*; Mr. E. Richardson, for Figs. 11, 24, 25, 46, 47, 48, 95, 96, 100, 108; Mr. A. J. Roberts, for Figs. 2, 66; the late T. E. Routh, for Figs. 40, 87, 88, 90, 103, 105, 111; Mr. H. J. Smith, for Fig. 29; the late Will F. Taylor, for Figs. 3, 5, 17, 31, 37, 41, 44, 49, 50, 53, 55, 58, 59, 61, 62, 65, 68, 71, 78, 79, 86, 91, 92, 93, 102, 104, 106, 107, 112, 115, 116; Messrs. The Topical Press Agency, Ltd., for Fig. 26; Mr. Edgar Ward, for Fig. 8; Miss Dorothy Whitburn, for Fig. 83; and Mr. Reece Winstone, F.R.P.S., for Fig. 57.

The frontispiece is reproduced by kind permission of Mr. Douglas Percy Bliss, M.A., A.R.C.A., and the line drawing on page 105 by permission of Mr. Hugh Mottram, A.R.I.B.A.

FOREWORD

Men pass away, but people abide. See that ye hold fast to the heritage we leave you. Yea, and teach your children its value, that never in the coming centuries their hearts may fail them or their hands grow weak. Hitherto we have been too much afraid, henceforth we will fear only God.—FRANCIS DRAKE, *quoted in the regimental orders of the 1st Glider Pilot Regiment.*

IN pouring rain I went to the Agricultural Show to see some Cheshire cheeses. It was my private opinion that for far too long had we people of England been compelled to endure cheese of the mouse-trap variety, and that doled out only in scanty portions, and I wished to observe whether the post-war cheeses augured of better things to come. A man who ought to know had been telling me that what with shortage of labour, fixed prices, and milk supplies rigidly controlled, it would be ten years at least before English cheeses came into their own again. So with ten thousand other people I braved the rain and mud, and tramped past challenge cups and goblets and some beautiful beasts belonging to the Duke of Westminster, to look at some cheeses. Yes, there they all were, a hundred and fifty of them, and though they were not the cheeses of former days, portly, matured nine months and blue-veined, they certainly made a fine sight. There was something solid and satisfying about the look of them, so that for a moment one forgot this curious post-war world in which we find ourselves in the pleasant surprise at discovering how this country craft had staged a come-back. If you are also one of those simple souls to whom some bread and cheese and a glass of cider constitutes a satisfying meal then you will understand this feeling.

My faith restored, I went out into the rain again, and as I travelled eastward along the modern highway which has superseded grass-grown Watling Street I felt a sudden desire to discover how other aspects of country life in this area had emerged from the turmoil of the past seven years. How was this North Midland countryside in general settling down to post-war conditions? Any attempt at delineating existing conditions would have but transitory value, but out of the mosaic of contemporary events surely one could attempt to fashion some slight contemporary record.

This wet, green Cheshire landscape through which I was passing, for instance; it did not appear to have come out of the war so badly. It still fulfilled Rupert Brooke's conception:

> White mist above the black hedgerows;
> The slumbering Midland plain;
> The silence where the clover grows, and dead leaves in the rain—
> Certainly these remain.

ix

Much of the land is grazed, and its pattern of hedgerows and dry-stone walls remains practically unimpaired by the passing of the years. Here were meadows and pastures, fields of oats, swedes and mangolds, as rich as any that could be found within reach of Mersey-side. Further east, on the moorlands of the Peak District, the grazing of sheep and young cattle continued, and probably would continue while world famine threatened. Even the open-field system at Laxton, in Nottinghamshire, still continued, and I was glad to learn from the local Executive Officer that he would resist very strongly any attempt to do away with this interesting survival from medieval times.

A little while later I went south again, and travelled through the Potteries and along the fringes of the Black Country to the green Vale of Trent, and then through Sherwood Forest to the Derwent Valley and so back to Manchester. On the way I observed with quizzical eyes the various factors which are shaping present-day England. Though the scars made by high explosives and incendiaries were green again, memorials of the war still remained in the form of abandoned airfields, surplus war factories and military training areas. Of those vast expanses of concrete from which our air fleets sailed away to liberate Europe, the Lord Chancellor has declared that it would cost up to £200,000 to restore an average site, and even then huge unsightly dumps of broken concrete would be left. It has been suggested instead that the Government acquire and develop these sites as holiday camps or in connection with their planning schemes.

Uses have already been found for some of the war factories, such as that at Swynnerton, in north Staffordshire, where ammunition is being broken down to recover the steel, brass and copper, which can be used for making electrical fittings. At the former Royal Ordnance factory at Radway Green gas and electric cookers and refrigerators are being manufactured. I was informed that the production target for this former shell-filling factory was 2,000 cookers and 500 refrigerators a week. The series of war factories engaged in light engineering and aircraft work may prove a valuable addition to the economy of the Potteries. It is suggested that the smaller china manufacturers might combine to take over an aircraft factory near Stoke, the factory being divided into units on the lines of a trading estate, firms sharing facilities such as transport, canteens and engineering workshops.

It took a war to teach us the part that buildings play in our lives, the power they possess the elevate or depress our spirits. Remember what Shaw wrote in one of his Prefaces? "The horrible murk and grime of the Pottery towns is caused by indifference to a stupid waste of sunlight, natural beauty, cleanliness and pleasant air, combined with a brutish appetite for money." The feature of the Potteries which the casual visitor notices most is the extremely poor living and working conditions; a large proportion of existing houses appear ripe for demolition. In the case of Stoke it has been suggested that the large shell-filling factory situated some distance from the main built-up area might perhaps be made the centre of a comprehensive redevelopment of the town, and that a large part of the town might be removed to the new site.[1]

Certainly we are in for a spate of building such as has never before been seen in England, and the shortage of houses is so acute that one can understand why many people argue that it does not matter where new buildings are put provided they are built as quickly as possible. People without homes are in no mood for arguments. Yet it was by precisely such reasoning that for years before the war the big industrial centres dumped their surplus populations on the neighbouring countrysides. The towns reached out into the farmlands, spreading built-up areas of roads, houses and factories, to the detriment of agriculture and natural amenities. This was part of the policy, or lack of policy, which, by crushing death duties on land, subsidised imports of foreign food and indifference to English farming, caused the decay of English agriculture and the breaking up of many large estates. With them went much of the essential beauty of England, and lovely houses were pulled down and sold piecemeal to speculative contractors.

A policy of taking land in payment of death duties is now in operation, such estates as are taken over to be administered, it appears, by the National Trust. This organisation already owns a good deal of land in the Peak District, notably in and about Dovedale, Edale and the Derwent Valley. As I write this, the radio has announced the formation of twelve great national parks, covering 5,682 square miles of England and Wales, while twelve other areas of outstanding beauty are to be protected. The scenic area with which this book is naturally most concerned is the Peak District, for it may not be generally realised that some twenty million people, not far short of half the population of England and Wales, live within sixty miles of the Peak. It is good news indeed that this lovely hill country is to be preserved as part of our scenic heritage, for to date it has happily suffered but little from industrialisation. (Though in 1938 the hill districts of Derbyshire contributed nearly three-quarters of the national output of twenty million tons of limestone, and you can't do that for long without some damage to the natural features of a countryside.)

But there is another side to this National Park idea, and

[1] *Prospects of the Industrial Areas of Great Britain*, by M. P. Fogarty (Methuen & Co., Ltd., 1945).

chatting with local people I found some who were not so keen on the proposal. "We should have hordes of wardens and rangers all over the place, and notices stuck up everywhere telling us we must not do this or that," one local resident commented. More to be feared, I should imagine, are the activities of the military authorities, whose presence is realised often only when sign-boards marked "W.D. Land. Keep Out" suddenly make their appearance in unsuspected places. For some years to come people will probably be reporting the discovery of unexploded ammunition on the moors. Mr. G. B. H. Ward, of the Sheffield Clarion Ramblers, in the chatty little handbook which he has edited for the past forty-six years, cites numerous instances of wanton damage done by soldiers, among them the remark made by an artillery non-com. who declared his intention of "knocking hell out of that," the object in question being Carl Wark, one of the most remarkable examples of a pre-historic fortress in the Midlands.

Of the question of access to the moorlands, of which I have written elsewhere, there is nothing fresh to add, for the new National Parks Bill will probably render any comment out of date.

I am writing this in a rambling old house which stands beside a dark little river; once it was a water-mill but now it is one of those newest of all hostelries, a youth hostel. In the yard outside our door a group of young people, sensibly clad in nothing much, are strolling about, talking or reading. There is a fresh, healthy, happy look about them, and a vivacity and zest for life which puts to shame the pessimistic remarks made by old women of both sexes that the young people of to-day aren't what they were in their young days. In their hands rests the biggest job of all, of making the new England which will gradually arise from the remnants of the old, and one wonders what they will make of this modern world of controls, of conscription, of prefabs, squatters, paid holidays and "Work or Want" posters. Surely young people who did their share to win a war can be trusted to do their share to win a peace?

For their benefit I prefaced this Foreword with some words of Francis Drake's, and for their benefit also I will finish with some words uttered by another great Englishman, words that are as true to-day as ever they were. They were spoken by John Milton when England was undergoing the greatest tribulation in her history, the Civil War:

Lords and Commons of England, consider what nation whereof ye are . . . a nation not slow and dull, but of a quick and piercing spirit, acute to invent, subtle and sinewy to discourse, not beneath the reach of any point, the highest that human capacity can soar to.

Brave words! What Milton will sing of England in her present hour?

2 WINTRY SUNSHINE ON MASSON HILL,
   MATLOCK, DERBYSHIRE

3   THE GATEHOUSE (MID-SIXTEENTH CENTURY), LITTLE MORETON HALL, CHESHIRE

(THE PROPERTY OF THE NATIONAL TRUST)

I

GENERAL SURVEY:
THE LAND AND THE PEOPLE

WHAT impression does the phrase "North Midland Country" convey to you? If suddenly asked this question the average person, especially the southerner, is apt to think of Crewe railway junction, the Potteries (12), the coalfields and ironworks of the Black Country, perhaps of Burton and its beers if his taste lies that way. But on the whole the region has a reputation synonymous for dirt and smoke and industry.

A rambler whom I encountered on the moors above our farm near the Staffordshire border expressed this typical view. "I've been wandering about these confounded hills for hours, trying to find the right path back to the railway," he told me. "I didn't know the Midlands could be so wild. I thought it was all industrial." He came from London, and his was a common view. Now he knows that though the North Midlands have some of the largest and smokiest industrial areas in the country they also possess much scenery of the type known as "typically English."

It must be admitted that the traveller's usual introduction to the region does not show him its best side. "Humph, the Midlands," travellers from the south are apt to say with a sniff, as their train approaches Stoke-on-Trent or Crewe, and they see the beginnings of that smoky pall which seems to stretch across the countryside all the way to Lancashire. To them it connotes a region of dull, depressing towns, where the people speak in broader, less-modulated tones than those in the south, and life and manners are more rough and ready. But to the city-sick people who every week-end swarm in their thousands out of Sheffield, Manchester and other industrial centres, out into the green woodlands of Nottinghamshire and Cheshire or the high hills of Derbyshire or Staffordshire, the phrase means something different. To them the North Midlands is a place of escape, a solace and a sanctuary. The truth lies somewhere between these two viewpoints.

For the purpose of this book I am considering the North Midlands as that part of England enclosed by Cheshire, Derbyshire, Staffordshire, Nottinghamshire and Leicestershire. It also takes in odd corners of Shropshire and Warwickshire and perhaps the whole of Rutland. No part of England has a character so difficult to assess as this group of loosely united counties. They do not fit into a mould as do, say, East Anglia, the North, or the West Country. They consist of so many dissimilar elements; Cheshire is a border county and looks toward Wales, Derbyshire is Pennine country which has somehow strayed into the green heart of the Midlands, Staffordshire is clannish and aloof, only "the Shires" seem to belong there. Ever since the days of Mercia, the middle kingdom of Saxon England, this region has remained elusive, a sort of buffer state between north and south. Even to-day many people regard it merely as a place which they cross in order to get to somewhere else. The North Midlands has no clearly defined boundaries, and because of this deficiency there is not that regional consciousness which, for example, makes a Wessex man proud to be a Wessex man. The Midlanders are county-proud, but that is all.

The truth is that England is divided less into counties than it is into districts. There are a great number of these districts, which often derive their names from topographical features or old-time political and ecclesiastical divisions. Some are named after ancient royal forests, others because of an industry or sport peculiar to that area, still others for a certain style of architecture, or because of literary or historical associations. Such names spring readily to mind—the Forest of Dean, the Fens, the Craven District of Yorkshire, the Hardy Country, the Vale of Evesham. Similarly, the North Midland region consists of a group of districts whose names are household phrases: the Peak District (34, 35), the Cheshire Plain (15), the Potteries (12), and the Black Country, Sherwood Forest (5) and the Dukeries, and the fox-hunting district of the Shires (4).

On the whole the North Midlands consists of fertile, rolling country, well wooded and watered, predominantly agricultural, but with areas which are among the most industrialised in England. Geologically it consists of an arc of red sandstone curving about the gritstone-limestone combination of the Peak District; the industrial areas mark the coal measures and ironstone workings. This region is the real heart of England, the source of much of its wealth. It has always been a focal point of political and economic unrest, for its people are a sturdy, independent type, apt to be suspicious of old ways merely because they are old. It was near Himley in Staffordshire that the Gunpowder Plot conspirators were besieged and captured. Nottingham saw the beginning of the Luddite Riots, when in 1811 thousands of unemployed textile workers began

4   A MEET OF THE RUFFORD HOUNDS, MAPLEBECK, NOTTINGHAMSHIRE

5   BILHAY, SHERWOOD FOREST, NOTTINGHAMSHIRE

destroying the new stocking frames and lace-making machinery. They made themselves masters of the town, seized arms, offered a reward for the capture of the mayor, and in the end seven regiments had to be drafted in to subdue them. Eighteen-seventeen saw the abortive Pentrich Rebellion in Derbyshire, when a group of unemployed labourers, stocking-makers and weavers, led by Jeremiah Brandreth, made a forlorn attempt to better their half-starved condition. They did some damage to property and accidentally shot a man before they were rounded up by the troops. The Government's ideas on reform consisted in having Brandreth and the other leaders hanged and beheaded.

In those dark days of the Industrial Revolution the plight of the English labourer was terrible, as Cobbett comments in caustic fashion:

"Leicester is a very fine town; spacious streets, fine inns, fine shops, and containing, they say, thirty or forty thousand people. It is well stocked with gaols, of which a new one, in addition to the rest, has just been built, covering three acres of ground. And as if proud of it, the grand portal has little turrets in the castle style, with embrasures in miniature on the caps of the turrets. Nothing speaks the want of reflection in the people so much as the self-congratulation which they appear to feel in these edifices in their several towns. Instead of expressing shame at these indubitable proofs in the increase of misery and crime, they really boast of these improvements as they call them. Our forefathers built abbeys and priories and churches, and they made such use of them that gaols were nearly unnecessary. We, their sons, have knocked down the abbeys and priories, suffered half the parsonage's houses and churches to pretty nearly tumble down, and made such use of the remainder that gaols and treadmills and dungeons have now become the most striking edifices in every county in the kingdom."

The building of new gaols was the authorities' reply to demands for reforms to relieve the hunger and economic distress caused by the introduction of labour-saving machinery and the enclosure of the common lands. Poverty was considered a crime, and any attempt to alleviate it was an unwarrantable interference with the natural laws of existence. No wonder that such an inhuman attitude aroused Cobbett's honest indignation.

"You have nothing to do but to walk through these villages to see the cause of the increase of the gaols. Standing on the hill at Knighton, you see the three ancient and lofty and beautiful spires rising up at Leicester; you see the river winding down through the broad bed of the most beautiful meadows man ever set eyes on; you see the bright verdure covering all the land, even to the tops of the hills, with here and there a little wood, as if made by God to give variety to the beauty of the scene, for the river brings the coal in abundance, for fuel, and the earth gives the brick and tile in abundance. But go down into the villages, invited by the spires, rising up amongst the trees in the dells, at scarcely even more than a mile or two apart: invited by these spires, go down into these villages, see the parson's house, large and in the midst of pleasure gardens; and then look at the miserable sheds in which the labourers reside! Look at these hovels, made of mud and straw; bits of glass, or old off-cast windows, without frames or hinges frequently, but merely stuck in the mud wall. Enter them and look at the bits of chairs or stools; the wretched boards tacked together to serve for a table; the floor of pebble, broken brick, or of the bare ground; look at the thing called a bed; and survey the rags on the backs of the wretched inhabitants; and then wonder if you can that the gaols and the dungeons and the treadmills increase, and that a standing army and barracks are become the favourite establishments in England."

Leicester to-day is a far different city, and Cobbett, were he alive, would be surprised to learn that the League of Nations had declared it to be the most prosperous city in the British Empire and the second most prosperous community in Europe.

HILL FARMS

The Peak District has always been one of the most individual parts of England. It is Pennine country, and though the people live in the Midlands they are not of them. They are a breed by themselves, always isolated and independent. Here in the deep wooded valleys, and among the bleak, wet moors, the little towns and villages and lonely farms remain untouched and unspoiled. Here is some of the wildest and loneliest hill-country in all England, miles-long stretches of heather, moss, and wimberry, where it was possible only a year or so ago for three girls to be lost for five days in the snow (they were still alive when found). A roadside sign near Rainow states: "Here John Turner was cast away in a heavy snowstorm in the year 1735. The print of a woman's shoe was found by his side in the snow where he lay dead." Each year the moorlands claim their victims.

The Peak District belies its name, for actually it is a flat-topped plateau of millstone grit, adjoining a lower plateau of carboniferous limestone. It has nine summits over 2000 feet set in rather bleak moorland, of heather and peaty bogs, slashed by rapid streams into steep ravines. The moorlands are forbidden territory to the general public, being preserved for shooting, and battles often take place between the gamekeepers and ramblers who refuse to be kept out.

HADDON HALL, DERBYSHIRE: A BIRD'S-EYE VIEW

The limestone provides spectacular cliffs and gorges, of which the high "tors" of Matlock and Chee Dale (14) are fine examples. But grandest of all is Dovedale (6), finer even than Cheddar Gorge, those miles of cliffs and woodlands, rocky crags and pinnacles, and gently falling waters. There is not even a road to desecrate its grandeur, and those who would see its wonders must walk. The limestone is famous for its caverns (35), Odin and Blue John and the Devil's Hole, whose underground paths and streams provide plenty of scope for the devotees of the sport of "potholing," sometimes designated by the appalling term of speleologists, just as fungus-lovers are called mycologists. This district is also noted for its possession of two of the finest mansions in England, Chatsworth House (54) and Haddon Hall (page 5). Some of the villages still keep up their old picturesque customs, the curfew, the sheep-dog trials on Longshaw Moor, well-dressing at Tissington (39), the Shrove Tuesday football match at Ashbourne.

It is a country of small farms, forty to a hundred and fifty acres, family owned and worked: grey stone farmhouses and outbuildings which blend into the grey-green of the hillsides. The people are a reserved, clannish folk, slow to make friends with strangers, yet staunch company once you are accepted. I remember a remark of Mr. Crichton Porteous' concerning the people of his valley: "I've been living here twelve years now, and the people are just beginning to regard me as though I have a right to be here."

One winter, the report goes, a hiker was taken ill on the moors, so his friend left him lying in the snow while he went to the nearest farmhouse for help. It is said that the farmer replied that it was no concern of his if folks were daft enough to go tramping in such weather, and if they could not look after themselves they ought to stay at home. The hiker went back to his companion and was helping him to stagger on a little further when the sick man collapsed and died in the snow. But all farmers are not so hard. Yet during my first winter in the hill country, when I lived alone in a little cabin which was snowbound for two or three weeks at a time, doing part-time work on a neighbouring farm, during all that cruel winter I was never once asked to step inside the farmhouse door. Sometimes the road to town, seven miles away, was blocked by snow for a week or more, and the milk-lorries could not get through. Then the "winter road" would come into existence, a sledge track zigzagging from farm to farm across the hills, with teams of horses hauling sledges loaded with churns. When the road was free of snow the hill people spoke of it as being "liberated."

In the valleys they go in for milk and rearing store cattle, sometimes egg production on a fairly large scale; the bleak uplands are suited only for sheepwalks. They grow roots, kale, and oats, which

6   TISSINGTON SPIRES, DOVEDALE, DERBYSHIRE

7   LICHFIELD CATHEDRAL, STAFFORDSHIRE:
LOOKING TO THE NAVE FROM THE SOUTH TRANSEPT

are mown green for silage. The light loamy soil can grow very good oats, and now, since 1940, it is showing that it can grow wheat as well. A field over a thousand feet above sea level, originally a cow pasture, last year produced twenty-five tons of oats on its twenty acres. Good potatoes have also been grown above the thousand-foot line, in fields that were formerly covered with gorse. Cattle are not turned out to grass until the end of May. With us haymaking comes late, and sometimes we don't cart the last load into the barns until half-way through September; remote farms high up in the hills are even later. One thing distinguishes the hill people from the people of the plain: in the hills they shoot the fox, down on the plain they hunt him with horse and hound.

The hill people's speech is akin to the Pennine dialects further north, but with a local flavour which spreads into neighbouring Staffordshire and Cheshire. *Tit* for horse, *rook* for a heap or mound, *bank* for hill, *pikel* for pitchfork; *bug-blinding* is whitewashing. *Wench* for woman, and *youth* for man are common forms of address. A curious word is *mexnin* (i.e., mixening or middening), meaning to muck-out shippons and stables. They have a sardonic sense of humour, and every farmer seems to possess a store of anecdotes and sayings. Here are some of them. "What do you know?" a miller asked a boy. "Only one thing," the boy replied. "What's that?" "That millers always have fat pigs." "And what don't you know?" "Whose bags of corn they are fed out of."

A young farmer joined the army and told his tailor to put a metal plate inside his uniform where his heart would be. When the uniform was ready he found the plate fixed to the seat of his trousers. "Why did you put it there?" he asked the tailor. "I wanted it over my heart." "Never been in the army before, have you?" the tailor asked him. "No." "Well, I have, and when the shooting starts that is where your heart will be."

A young lad was apprenticed to a farmer for twenty years. He had only been there a fortnight when the farmer kicked him. "Never mind," said the lad to himself. "I've only got another nineteen years, eleven months, and two weeks, and then I can tell him what I think of him." Then there was the man who had trained his donkey to live on less, and less, and he had just trained it to live on nothing at all when it went and died on him.

CHESHIRE FOLK

The hills drop steeply toward the Cheshire Plain (15), and we pass almost at once from a country of drystone walls to one of hedges and ditches. But north-eastern Cheshire is part of the Peak District, with hills nearly 2000 feet high. The cotton-spinning industry of Lancashire overlaps into Cheshire and the little foothill towns around Stockport and Macclesfield fostered many minor industries. Kettleshulme was one of the few places in England where candle-wicks were made, until the industry was abandoned in 1937. Disley was the capital of the skewer and spindle trade, which explains the presence of the great number of ash trees in this district. Peat is still dug at Alderley Edge, while near Rowarth some unemployed colliers started working their own coal mine.

In these towns you come across a form of spontaneous entertainment known as "chumming up." Whenever a crowd gathers in a public house, park, or even while sheltering from the rain in a tramway shelter, it is the custom for everybody present to take their turn at entertaining the others, either by singing a song, telling a story, reciting, or playing an instrument. This is cabaret in its original form, casual and unrehearsed, done solely for their own amusement. Here is a story told by one of these impromptu entertainers:

"Dosta see yon couple, Sam and Liz, going down street? Aye, well, did ever hear tell how near they came to not getting wed? It were like this now. One day about a week before wedding Sam comes to Liz and he says: 'Liz, Ah've gotten some news for thee. Ah'm no going to wed thee.' 'Whatever arta saying, tha big gawp,' says Liz. 'Why, weddings only a week off and all t'presents have come.' 'Ah dunna care, Ah'm no going to wed thee,' says Sam. 'Ah've changed me mind.' 'Well, tha will look an awful foo' and folks will talk, tha knows,' says Liz. 'It conna be helped,' says Sam. 'Ah've changed me mind, Ah tell thee.' So Liz thinks a bit and then she says: 'Well, if tha's changed tha mind it conna be helped, Ah suppose. But Ah'll not have thee made a fool of before all t'folks, Ah luv thee too much. Ah'll tell thee what we'll do. We'll say nowt to nobody, and on day of wedding parson chap will say: "Sam, come thee here, lad—now dosta want to tak' this woman to be tha lawful wedded wife?" and you mun say, "I will." Then he'll say to me: "Liz, dosta want this man to be tha lawful wedded husband?" and I'll say "No!" and then folks will think it's all my fault, and tha'll not look such a fool.' So Sam thinks it over a bit and then he says: Aye, that's a reet good idea, Liz. We'll do it.' So day of wedding comes and parson chap he calls out to Sam: 'Now, Sam, wilta tak' this woman to be tha lawful wedded wife?' so Sam says: 'Aye, tha's reet—yes—Ah mean—Ah will.' Then he says to Liz: 'Now, Liz, wilta tak' this man to be tha lawful wedded husband?' 'Aye,' says Liz. 'I will.' So Sam nudges her and says: 'Tha big gawp, tha's gone and said wrong thing. Tha should have said "No."' 'Eh, lad,' says Liz. 'Tha's not the only person who can change tha mind. I changed my mind too.' And that's how they were wed."

8 STONE WALLS AND FIELD STRIPS, LITTON, DERBYSHIRE

[*From a lithograph by J. Flower, c.* 1830

9   HIGH CROSS STREET, LEICESTER

[*From an engraving after T. Allom,* 1841

10   THE MARKET PLACE AND ST. DIONYSIUS' CHURCH,
MARKET HARBOROUGH, LEICESTERSHIRE

But it is the Plain by which Cheshire is known best; the rich, grassy landscapes which are typical of dairying country. This is a very different world from the grim uplands of the Peak. Here are farmhouses built of local red sandstone weathered to a mellow grey-brown, slate roofs, Dutch barns and comely haystacks in the open fields. Old-world villages of half-timbered houses and black-and-white manors nestle along winding lanes between green meadows where somnolent cattle graze. Placid, reed-fringed meres, often of considerable extent, constitute a miniature lakeland. The arable farms of Cheshire are found chiefly on the rich, sandy loam. They usually follow a four-course rotation; a root crop, usually potatoes, two cereal crops, usually oats, though of late years wheat has come more into favour, and grass for either one or two years. Rye used to be a crop of some importance. It was threshed by hand to avoid crushing the straw, and was used for packing in the Potteries.

Early potatoes are produced for the big industrial markets, as the sandy soil of Cheshire appears less liable to frost than Lancashire. Vegetables are supplied by the market gardens in the Mersey Valley, though this type of intensive cultivation is commoner further west in the Wirral Peninsula. But Cheshire is, above all, the county of the dairy farmer, and up to the outbreak of the war parts of it and of north Staffordshire had 95 per cent. of the land under permanent grass. Probably no county in England was more heavily stocked with cattle. Now, of course, owing to the activities started by Mr. Hudson and his colleagues, the lush green pastures have changed into a mosaic of cornfields and green crops.

Cheese and salt were the earliest staple industries of Cheshire. The Salt Field occupies the central portion of the county, along the River Weaver, where agriculture suddenly gives way to a vigorous industrial development. Northwich, Middlewich, and Winsford, towns built on the salt, are among the queerest-looking in England, for owing to the continual subsidence switchback streets and leaning houses present a bizarre appearance. Buildings which vanish out of sight, and lakes which suddenly appear overnight are commonplace stories in this area. In 1933 a hole fifty feet wide and three hundred feet deep suddenly opened up near the river. The Salt Museum in Northwich is unique.

Out of the flat plain beyond the river rises a series of steep sandstone escarpments, 600 feet high, known as the Beeston and Peckforton Hills. Clothed in dark woodlands, their summits crowned by ancient castles, these hills form one of the most picturesque regions of England. The 4000 acres of Delamere Forest form a great arc of woodland round the saddleback ridge of Eddisbury Hill, crowned by the great ramparts of an Iron Age fortress.

NMC : C

In the autumn of 1938 I formed one of a party of unemployed
men, who under the guidance of Mr. W. J. Varley and students from
Liverpool University, excavated the ruins on the hilltop. The
original fortress had been built by people belonging to the second
wave of Celtic migration from Europe, the Brythonic Celts from
whom the Welsh derived their language. It is believed they were
an upland people, and as the Roman advanced toward the lower
Severn they followed the hill ranges from Shropshire into Cheshire.
(Pottery which was dug up resembled the earliest Iron Age pottery
of south-east England, thus demonstrating what was previously
guessed at, that types of pottery made in that part of England as
early as the fourth century before Christ continued to be made
in the remote north-west up till the eve of the Roman conquest.)
They settled here in the first century before Christ, and later, perhaps on the eve of the Roman conquest, the fort had been enlarged
and strengthened. But the fort was unable to stem the Roman
advance; the invaders had destroyed the ramparts, filled up the
ditches, and blocked or dismantled the entrances.

According to the Mercian Register (which is actually a document
incorporated in the Anglo-Saxon Chronicle), Ethelfleda, the warlike daughter of King Alfred, built a "burh" or town on Eddisbury
in 914. It was our ambition to discover remains of this settlement,
but though we dug for several weeks, through layers representing
half a dozen different cultures, we found no trace of the town.
But we did lay bare the Celtic fortifications; ramparts twenty feet
high with firebays and dug-outs as in a modern trench system;
V-shaped rock-hewn ditches with sharpened stakes on which
invaders were impaled; sunken entrances spanned by oaken gates,
with guard-chambers on either side, camouflaged with drystone
walling to mislead an invading force; surprisingly modern was the
work of these Iron Age military engineers. And though we did not
know their name or history, we could see here how they had lived,
the tools they had used and the hearths at which they had done
their cooking. I slept one night in a guard-chamber by the main
gate of the fortress, a unique experience few men can have undergone, and was awakened at midnight by a big man armed with a
long sword. Was he a ghost, I wonder?

Beyond the sandstone ridges the green meadows slope down
toward the River Dee, a salmon river, where even the lordly sturgeon
has been taken upon occasion. Chester is the finest example of a
walled town to be found in England. North-westward stretches the
Wirral Peninsula, like the spout of a teapot, a low, undulating land
fringed by sandhills and marshes; submerged forests warn us that the
land is slowly sinking into the sea.

11 ECTON HILL IN THE MANIFOLD VALLEY, STAFFORDSHIRE, WITH WETTON MILL IN THE FOREGROUND

12   THE OUTSKIRTS OF A POTTERY TOWN: STOKE-ON-TRENT, STAFFORDSHIRE

BLACK COUNTRY

The Cheshire Plain continues into north Shropshire and Stafford-shire. This is a district of heavy soils, thick boulder clay, and is mainly devoted to dairy farming. It is pleasant undulating country, where the substantial farms and villages cluster about old red sand-stone churches and black and white, half-timbered manor houses. In the keuper marl district of mid-Staffordshire they go in for cereals and root crops, and supply the huge industrial populations to the south with milk. North Staffordshire is wild and rugged, and its rocky hills and deep, wooded valleys contain some of the finest scenery in all England. Whoever has followed the River Manifold from source to mouth, or tramped those strange hills known as the Five Clouds, or seen Alton Towers like a Rhineland castle on its rock, will know how this country can grip the heart of the beholder. Further south lies Cannock Chase, 30,000 acres of heath and wood-land, still largely rural despite the growth of the collieries.

But those who know Staffordshire only by reputation think of the dirt and smoke of her industrial centres rather than of the beauty of her countryside. It is by the Potteries, the Black Country (30), and Birmingham (which it shares with Warwickshire) that the county is best known. The Potteries are the "Five Towns" familiar to readers of Arnold Bennett's novels. Potteries have been estab-lished here since the seventeenth century, but it was in 1759 that Josiah Wedgwood (32) founded his works at Etruria, the home of the finest pottery in England. Once there really were five towns, but in 1910 they amalgamated to form Stoke-on-Trent, which, with a population of 300,000, now forms the largest town in the county. It was the largest experiment in local self-government which has ever taken place. In *The Old Wives' Tale* and *Clayhanger* Bennett has immortalised the district; he saw the sombre beauty of it, where other people saw only the sordidness. He writes of "the Indian-red architecture of Burslem (31)—tall chimneys and rounded ovens, schools, the scarlet market-place. The sedate reddish-browns and reds of the composition, all netted in flowing scarves of smoke, harmonised exquisitely with the chill blues of the chequered sky."

But it is true that there are few more ugly and depressing places than these industrial towns of the Midlands. It is not perhaps realised how far back dates Birmingham's record as a centre of active metal-working, and just because a number of little industries developed from the old days of domestic handwork each little place has its own separate industry (*v.* page 28). A number of these, like the making of chains and nails at Cradley, were till comparatively recently carried on under terribly sweated conditions. "Where there's smoke there's brass," they used to tell me when I was a lad in Lancashire, and this philosophy of ugliness seems to have been common to all industrial centres. With the coming of the Industrial Revolution streets of monotonous and depressing houses were run up with infinite repetition by the acre, and the whole effect is, of course, entirely amorphous. See them from the cab of a transport lorry at night, the gigantic factories with their chimneys belching smoke and sparks, the winding gear at the pitheads, the flames from the furnaces, the innumerable railway lines and dirty canals, the endless rows of dismal houses and squalid streets, and you will reflect anew over D. H. Lawrence's remark that though spiritually the English were the salt of the earth, in the contriving of their habitations they were more ignominious than rabbits. What a great portion of England is now getting further and further removed from the "green and pleasant land" of the story-books.

Repellent though they may be to a countryman, yet life stirs in these towns; in much of England further south you get the impression that history has come to an end. The future is not settled here, as in other districts. Birmingham, more than any other city in England, reminded me of Canada. London, Liverpool, Manchester seemed stereotyped, but Birmingham had that same restless "frontier" spirit which characterises the New World. In the construction of its new houses (rarely were two alike), in the dress and manner of its inhabitants, it expressed individuality, restless and dissatisfied, often crude, born of the many diverse elements still being drawn into its grimy maw. Five generations of industrialism has produced in this region a people of strongly marked character, for class distinctions were less binding here and it was possible for a man to become his own master. Then, too, the Midlands was the home of Nonconformity, and Wesleyans, Baptists, Congregationalists and other churches flourished. Because of these things the region is a melting-pot in which the people of half a dozen counties are being moulded into a new type.

The Black Country overlaps into Warwickshire, which here pokes a grimy finger into the North Midlands, reaching almost to Derbyshire.

THE SHIRES

Beyond the counties already mentioned lie the kindred shires of Nottingham and Leicester, a deeply rural region of untouched villages and little market towns, where life still moves at a placid, unhurried pace. This is "the Shires," land-minded and hunting-minded. Picture it as a broad, undulating plain, spanned by the small hill-ranges of the Wolds, where the chequerboard of wide green fields (17), dark spinneys and coverts, the staunch red brick farmhouses and old stone manors, the miles of blackthorn hedges, attest the solid agricultural virtues. Here is the home of Stilton cheese and Melton Mowbray pies. Solid, too, might be the adjective describing the people of the farmlands, slow of thought and speech, probably the most conservative, stick-in-the-mud element in England, with the possible exception of East Anglia. In several of the Wold villages the curfew still rings at sunset, as it has done for nearly a thousand years. Yet even here the countryside is changing, and villagers in remote places are becoming sophisticated. I remember once asking an old farm worker near Great Glen (how odd a name for a flat Leicestershire village!) what the weather was likely to be on the following day. "Oh, it will be fine," he replied. "Fine weather, indeed." "Now how can you tell that?' I asked him, thinking to learn something of weather lore. "Why, I heard it on the wireless, of course," was the prompt reply.

The history of the village labourer would lead one to expect a downtrodden and servile class of worker. In their book *The Village Labourer* the Hammonds have reminded those "who blame the supine character of the labourer" of the poverty and oppression his race has undergone. Yet I have worked on farms in half a dozen counties in England, and I find this far from being the case. The English farm labourer is a man of spirit and independence, and if he sets his mind on a thing all the boss's remonstrations cannot make him change it. Far from being downtrodden and servile he is always capable of telling the boss when he is wrong, and of sticking up for his own rights. This may be due to the fact that farming is fortunately one of the few remaining industries where this personal contact between employer and employed is still possible. Moreover, it is quite wrong to refer to the farm worker as a "labourer," for if any man is skilled it is he. A skilled carpenter or plumber would not thank you for calling him a labourer; neither does the farm worker. This much I have learned after several years working on the land, that even "singling" turnips is skilled work, and building hay and corn stacks is an art.

Those who think of the Shires as quite flat should see the rocky heights of Charnwood Forest (91, 92) in Leicestershire, towering 900 feet above the neighbouring coalfields. After agriculture and mining the staple industry is hosiery; Leicester, Loughborough and other towns have developed a prosperous industry since the invention of power-driven frames early in the nineteenth century. This area also produced the modern English town, of which Derby, Leicester and Nottingham are such good examples. The Roman cities fell into disuse, the Saxons did not build towns, so the modern English city had its origin in the five boroughs founded by the Danes. Instead of over-development or under-development you get respectably sized towns, each with its surrounding green belt, which contrast

favourable with the unplanned, congested areas of London, Lancashire or the Black Country.

From Leicester to near Uppingham the country consists of clay
land, the familiar grasslands of the dairy farmer. Milk floats unload-
ing churns at wayside platforms to await the arrival of the daily
lorry are a familiar feature, and the hedger working with mallet
and billhook is a sight strange to eyes accustomed to the drystone
walls of the uplands. On the clay they go in for sheep and cattle,
and you see very little ploughland (the war has changed that, of
course); the houses and villages have not the more opulent appearance of the farms situated on the more easily worked soils of Rutland.

The grass vales are famous fox-hunting country, and no district
of England has so many hunting-seats. "It is the only county
in the world," wrote one M.F.H., "that appears to have been
intended for fox-hunting and where fox-hunting can be seen in all
its glory." Melton Mowbray (102) and Market Harborough (10)
are the places to be visited in "the season." Fox-hunting was born
at Quorndon Hall, home of Hugo Meynell, during the latter part
of the eighteenth century. Meynell has been called the "Father of
English Fox-hunting," for though foxes had been hunted in England
from times immemorial he was the first person to systematically
develop it into an organised sport. Long before his death in 1808
he had firmly established the fox-hunting tradition in Leicestershire,
and now its Hunts, the Quorn (99), Pytchley, Cottesmore and
Belvoir (100), are famous wherever fox-hunters congregate.

This is not the place to argue the merits or demerits of the sport,
but the following extract from an article in *The Field*[1] epitomises
the hold which it has on its adherents.

"What is the one chief idea that we have been accustomed to
associate with a grass country and more especially with the honoured
name of Leicestershire, ever since we learned to hunt or even talk
of hunting? In what have we been taught to consider lies its first
charm, and what does experience tell us is its ruling delight? Is it
not the springy turf and firm elastic footing, the power of skimming
lightly over the surface, and bounding gaily over its fences—heeding
neither pace nor would-be obstacle, but revelling in their presence
and trusting to blood and courage to make light of them? Is it
not the dream of such a happiness that makes provincial youth to
groan, rebel against the toils that hold him and to hate his native
soil? Is it not the remembrance of such that will bring a flush to
the withered cheek and a sparkle to the dimming eye of the Rector,
as he tells how he flew the raspers side by side with the old Squire,
and held his horse as the other brushed a fox that had thought

---

[1] Capt. Pennel-Elmhirst, prominent figure in the Shires during the 70's and 80's of
last century.

13   MONSAL DALE, DERBYSHIRE

[Both from engravings after Joseph Farington, R.A., 1818

14   SCENE IN CHEE DALE, DERBYSHIRE

15 FARMING FIELD CHEQUERWORK, LITTLE LEIGH, CHESHIRE

himself invincible? Is it not for this that men lavish time and money, and think no sacrifice too great so long as they can be in this sphere to indulge in their all-absorbing pursuit?" That is the true fox-hunter speaking.

The attitude of the sportsman toward those who would restrict his activities is best shown in a letter from a nobleman living in London to his agent in Leicestershire.

"I must desire that all those tenants who have shown themselves friends to the several fox-hunts in your neighbouring counties— Lord Spencer's, the Duke of Rutland's, Mr. Meynell's and Lord Stamford's—may have the offer and refusal of their farms on easy and moderate terms. But those who destroy foxes or otherwise interrupt gentlemen's diversions—send me their names and addresses. . . . My sole object is the good of the community."

The Wold country pastures were long famed for the excellent wool they produced; it was known as the best in England and laid the foundations of the county's woollen industry. In the eighteenth century Robert Bakewell of Loughborough introduced the new Leicester type of sheep, and the county's reputation for high-grade wool was still further enhanced. To-day this breed is found wherever wool is extensively produced.

The undulating country continues into south Nottinghamshire where along the Trent and in the Vale of Belvoir is farmland as good as any in England. The old market town of Newark (112) marks the dividing line between the Wolds and the flat fenlands. In western Nottinghamshire the remnants of Sherwood Forest (5) screen the farmlands from the colliery districts in the Erewash Valley, on the Derbyshire border. For those who like an historical flavour the extensive wooded area of the Dukeries still retains something of the atmosphere of Robin Hood and his Merry Men, and the diligent traveller can uncover many associations with this semi-legendary figure. At Cresswell Crags is a cave which Robin Hood used, at Edwinstowe he and Maid Marian were married, at Fountain's Dale is the place where Friar Tuck lived, and you can still see the well into which Robin was tumbled after their epic fight.

Some of the villages about here contain curious and unique objects. Southwell (116), a "city" of only 3000 people, has in its cathedral an altar made of parts of aeroplanes shot down in the First World War. East Leake possesses a shawm, that curious musical instrument mentioned in the Bible, a great tin trumpet over eight feet long. Until 1855 it was used in church by the bass singers. Another village should be the small boys' Mecca, for it boasts a genuine, dyed-in-the-wool pirate flag.

But probably the most interesting place of all, to a countryman at any rate, is the village of Laxton, near Ollerton. It is the last place in England where the old open-field system of cultivation, general throughout the country in medieval times, is practised. Laxton is shut away from the world by winding lanes and barred gates, and to reach it I had to walk three miles of very stony road. The farm buildings are clustered together in the village, with the huge open fields stretching away on every side. It was my luck to encounter the schoolmaster, so I got him to explain the system to me.

"The principle of the open-field system is simple," he told me. "The ploughland is divided into three great open fields of about 300 acres each. Each year two of the three fields are cultivated, while the third remains fallow. Of the two that are cultivated, one is planted with wheat, the other with spring corn, which may be barley, oats, peas or beans. Now do you see anything curious about those men ploughing over there?"

I said I thought it strange that so many men should be needed to work one field.

"Ah, but they are not all working together," was the reply. "No farmer has his land all in one piece. That is where the medieval system differs from the modern. A tenant has his land allotted to him in ten strips, which may be scattered in any part of the two fields. The original idea of allotting the land this way was to ensure that each tenant shared the poor land as well as the good. Each strip is separated from its neighbour by a grass track which must not be ploughed up, even if a tenant has strips which lie side by side. These grassy tracks are called 'sykes,' and each one has a name, Sidelings Syke, Roebuck Syke, and so on. The right to cut hay from these sykes is auctioned off at haymaking time. The highest bidder for each syke puts a shilling in the pool, and after the sale this is spent in cheese and beer. When the crops have been harvested a day is fixed on which the whole stock of the village can be turned loose to graze on the stubble."

"But who decides how the strips shall be allotted?" I asked.

"The whole system is governed by the Court of the Manor which meets twice a year," he replied. "The bailiff summons the farmers to the court by ringing a bell, and if they fail to attend they are fined twopence. A jury of twelve men is then elected, which allots the strips and decides when the fields shall be declared open for grazing. The jury examines the fields in December to see that each farmer has looked after his strips. Farmers who do not keep their ditches clean or who leave soil on common grass are fined. Half the fines go to the lord of the manor, Earl Manvers, the other half is spent in beer for the jury. A jury once fined Earl Manvers himself for leaving a heap of soil on common grass."

We walked along the village street, which was lined with farm

buildings and haystacks attached to the houses, and presently came
to a small, stone-walled enclosure.

"This is the pinfold," remarked my guide. "Stock which have
strayed are put in here by the pinder, and the owner has to pay a
fine of fourpence to get them out."

I must add a footnote to his explanation. People who have
described this system as a communal type of farming are wrong
(except in the very loose sense that all men's activities together are
communal). These fields are in no sense communal in character,
for Laxton is part of the Manvers estate, and those who have
holdings in the open fields are tenants, as on any other estate.
Farming as we know it to-day is a fairly modern development, and
did not come about until all the open fields had been enclosed, and
the system of scattered strips had been replaced by compact individual holdings.

FOOTNOTE: THE FUTURE

One of the questions to be settled now the war is over is whether
or not the people of England shall be permitted more access to the
English countryside. At present so much of it is barred to them,
and the words "Trespassers will be prosecuted" are now inevitably
associated with English parks and woodlands. Private ownership
of great tracts of country, sporting interests, even such things as
Forestry Commissions and Water Boards which are supposed to
be the servants of the public and not its master, all these things
combine to keep English people from their national heritage. In
this brief survey of the districts comprising the North Midlands we
have seen that it contains some of the grandest and most beautiful
scenery in England. The trouble is that so much of it cannot be
visited by the ordinary Englishman and his wife. In much of the
Peak District grouse count for more than men, and the hills are
well guarded by gamekeepers who see that outsiders do not intrude.
Around Bleaklow Hill thirty-seven square miles are without a single
public footpath, and you venture there at your peril. Charnwood
Forest (91, 92) in Leicestershire is a range of hills ten miles long by
six miles wide, yet apart from the motor highways which cross it
practically the whole area is closed to the general public. Is it fair
that so much of the best of England should be barred to the people,
to suit the pleasure of the few? Now the feeling is growing up that
this state of affairs is not good enough, and that the people of
England should have the right to walk over their own land. We
have one of the most beautiful and fascinating countries in the world,
but what a lot of it we are never allowed to see. It is true that the
National Trust has managed to secure a number of historical spots

and open spaces, free of access to everybody, but they labour under difficulties, and a great deal more is required. Give the people of England the freedom of their own country.

But to be fair, we must also see the other side of the picture. I believe that people ought to have the right of access to the woods and open spaces of England, but I must admit that this can be a heart-breaking experience for those who have the interests of the English countryside at heart. How often have we land workers suffered from having gates left carelessly open, so that cattle strayed among growing corn, from thoughtless ramblers walking across grass ready for mowing, from picnic fires and lighted cigarette ends which set woodlands and hillsides ablaze. In the hill country on the borders of Cheshire and Staffordshire where I worked our greatest bugbear is that people will keep knocking down our drystone walls, for the sheer joy of seeing them roll into the river, or for making picnic seats and tables, or for enabling their dogs to burrow underneath for rabbits. Do you wonder that we hate trespassers? (In Ontario when I was a boy I have received a dose of buckshot in my backside for less than that.) Why, I have known them to knock down a drystone boundary wall in order to make stepping-stones across the river, and we had to work until eleven o'clock at night to rebuild it. And these were not childish hooligans, but grown-up responsible (?) adults, who had, presumably, received a good education. Now we do our best to keep people out of the woods.

It seems that public consciousness must be educated; people must be taught that the land is their own property, and that they must treat it decently. They would not like their homes to look like rubbish-tips; why then turn the countryside into one? They will learn, if shown how. When I came back to England from Canada I was amazed to see how all the public parks and gardens were walled or railed in, and surrounded by signs forbidding you to do this or that. Out in Ontario, where I was educated, there were no walls or railings round the parks and you were free to wander where you willed. Yet nobody stole the flowers or made a pig-sty of the place. Cannot England become the same? Give people the freedom of their country, but teach them that liberty does not mean licence. Make them understand that farmlands are places where some of the hardest work in the country is done, under difficult conditions, and that the possession of right of way across the countryside does not mean freedom to walk over growing crops, or to do as they please in woods and meadows. Only a fool would interpret freedom in that way. The job is to make the townsman country-conscious. How is it to be done?

But this question of access to the land is only one aspect of a much larger problem. As well as the England we love there is the

16 SPRING PLOUGHING, WOODHOUSE EAVES,
LEICESTERSHIRE

17 THE VALE OF BELVOIR AND THE WOLDS FROM
NETHER BOUGHTON HILL, LEICESTERSHIRE

[*After a drawing by A. Arnst*

18   THE MARKET PLACE, NOTTINGHAM, 1859

[*From a lithograph, c. 1840*

19   ST. PETER'S CHURCH SIDE, NOTTINGHAM

England we are not so proud of. The England that has been spoiled by slums (rural as well as urban), by ribbon-development and jerry-built housing estates, by the destruction of its woodlands and the pollution of its rivers, by slag heaps, by surface iron-mining which makes square miles of the countryside look as though a major war had been fought there; so much of England to-day is a sad memorial to years of ruthless exploitation in the sacred name of profits. Land-owners and industrialists have been free to engage in a crazy game of beggar-my-neighbour, without regard to the social consequences of their actions. This is the first and biggest problem; to take away from men such as these the power of destroying England for their private gain. Who is to own the land of England? In future public interest should come first. Private privileges and monopolies must learn the truth of Lord Chief Justice Coke's dictum: "How long so-ever it hath continued, if it be against reason it is of no force in law." Town and regional planning, the decentralisation of government and of industry, future agricultural policy, afforestation, compulsory labour service for youth, these things as well as the question of National Parks and access to the countryside are all linked together. With a population which is 80 per cent. urban, condemned to spend most of its life in the artificial atmosphere of modern industrial centres, it is imperative that some answer to these questions be found as speedily as possible.

I cannot do better than quote the concluding paragraph of a little booklet entitled *Your Inheritance*, published by the Housing Centre, the best shilling's worth I have come across for a long time:

"When people get sentimental they quote 'Our England is a garden.' Our England is *not* a garden. Or if it is the rubbish heap has run amok. But it might almost be thought of as a large, a very large, estate: run at the request of the life-tenants by 600 more or less carefully elected stewards (still mostly Whigs at heart). A big chance has come the way of the people on the estate, the biggest in its history. We must learn what is required of us. And then we must act. First a Survey—then a plan of action—*and then the action*, remembering that the distinction we have been in the habit of making between the beautiful country and the dreary town is false. The countryside is an industrial area, nice because our fathers took the trouble to make it so. We can make it as bad as our towns or our towns as good as our country."

II

TOWNS AND INDUSTRIES
THE DANISH BOROUGHS

" A GREAT scrabble of ugly pettiness over the face of the
land," is how D. H. Lawrence described English towns, and
though these are hard words it cannot be denied that they
are still largely true. We have the largest urban population in the
world, and some of the worst-looking towns you can meet with
anywhere. The North Midlands has its share of ugliness, showing
squalid industrialism at its worst, but in its three largest towns is
the nearest thing to a planned, spacious, comfortably sized *urb* that
we possess. Nottingham, Derby and Leicester seem bent on trans-
forming themselves into cities of the future. All three were founded
by the Danes and all became industrialised at a very early date.
Nottingham smiths were famous in the Middle Ages: Leicester was
a wool town in the thirteenth century: Derby numbered fourteen
mills in Domesday Book: but the turning point in their history was
the Industrial Revolution, and in particular the invention of various
spinning machines by Arkwright and Hargraves. Lace-making
brought Nottingham fame and prosperity while hoisery became one
of the two staple trades of Leicester (the making of a hundred
thousand pairs of boots each day is the other). Now both cities
have fifty or a hundred other trades as well.

The Midlands was the home of Nonconformity, and this restless,
energetic spirit was, during the nineteenth century, actively revo-
lutionary. Leicester was a Chartist stronghold, and it is significant
that only once during the early part of her long reign did Queen
Victoria visit the town; not for nothing was it known as the
"Metropolis of Dissent." The Midlanders made money from their
many innovations, and put up tangible evidence of their wealth in
the form of buildings, good solid Victorian Gothic which is now
presenting their descendants with sundry problems. After the First
World War the three towns decided to go modern. Nottingham
swept away the biggest open-air market in England (18), where

the traditional Goose Fair (24, 25) had been held for untold centuries, and built itself a magnificent civic centre instead. Derby also destroyed its old-fashioned market in order to make a bus station. Leicester has accomplished a feat which other towns might well emulate; it tore down the tangle of old streets and buildings and made a fine new roadway over half a mile long through the centre of the town; Charles Street is said to have cost a million pounds.

In fact they all seem to have gone rather heavily on civic centres and police stations; but some people may prefer a Goose Fair. Perhaps eventually they aim to have straight right-angled streets and semi-skyscrapers on the American model, but though I was bred among towns such as these I must confess I find them singularly uninspiring compared to winding English streets. But then, I'm no motorist! There has been a great effort at slum clearance and rehousing. A tremendous industrial upheaval as long as seventy-five years ago set Leicester pulling down her old property and housing people further out. Nottingham claims to have built more houses than any town of her size in England. Towns must grow; *how* they did it appears to have been nobody's business.

In the process of modernisation much that was old and fascinating has been swept away, and tidily minded councillors excuse such vandalism on the plea of modern efficiency. It was Leicester which nearly sacrificed one of the finest Roman baths in the country for the sake of building a new corporation bath-house. Derby is very disappointing in its historical remains; old houses, walls and gates, all are gone. It is true that we have in return a profusion of such things as, at Leicester, public lavatories and rubbish containers, but admirable though these are they are insufficient compensation for the destruction of much that was unique and lovely. This is not to decry the installation of public conveniences, the absence of which renders a visit to some towns very uncomfortable. And why don't towns erect more seats where you can sit down when you are tired; this would be a more sensible form of memorial than a statue which nobody looks at.

Perhaps I should absolve Leicester from some of these accusations, for it is the friendliest and most go-ahead town I know. Its City Information Bureau is an admirable institution which might well be copied by other towns. It's a very clean-looking place, is Leicester, and a good deal of the credit for this must go to the department which prevents factories from filling the town with smoke. It's a green city, too, for there are plenty of trees and open spaces. One of the best things about it is the New Walk (new perhaps when the Danes walked there), a mile-long promenade in the centre of the town where you can saunter undisturbed by motor traffic.

Though a place of great antiquity it would be possible for a casual visitor to pass through Leicester without realising that it possessed historical monuments quite unknown to other great industrial centres which, two centuries ago, were only unimportant villages. Much of the old medieval town remains a self-contained area undisturbed by the growth of modern Leicester about it (9). But unlike many towns Leicester does make some attempt to show off its ancient monuments. Where else can you see a Roman Forum in the heart of an English town? There is a local patriotism which makes Leicester men enthusiastically display the wonders of the place to visitors, aided and abetted by the aforementioned Information Bureau. Thus they will show you the Jewry Wall, which is now understood to be part of the Roman basilica—surely those battered stones *must* grip your imagination?—and the delightful Elizabethan Guildhall (23), where by pressing a button you can light up the dark prison cell where Quakers were confined in the bad old days. They will show you the Newarke Gate and the Tudor Gate, old chantry houses and any number of old churches—but why should I do the Information Bureau out of a job? Leicester Castle doesn't look in the least like a castle, but the baronial hall inside has been used continuously as a court of justice for over 600 years; it is a pity it is divided into separate courts, as it would look so much finer if these were removed. Anyway, do have a look at the Castle Green where the headsman's block stood and headless skeletons have been dug up.

The turret gateway leading to the castle was the scene of John Bunyan's conversion, for when a comrade who was doing sentry duty was killed in his place (this was during the siege of Leicester in the Civil War), Bunyan's thoughts immediately turned to the leading of a better life. But his is only one among many celebrated names, for King Lear and his daughters lived here, Wycliffe was here, and Chaucer was here; indeed, they will tell you a yarn that he was married at the church of St. Mary de Castro. The great Cardinal Wolsey lies buried somewhere among the ruins in Abbey Park, though he is now better remembered as a brand of underwear. Thomas Cook was here, too, for he ran his first excursion from Leicester station. Of the many old churches in the town St. Nicholas' is perhaps the most interesting for it contains Roman, Saxon, Norman and Early English masonry; it stands on the site of a pagan temple and Roman pillars still lie scattered about. The narrow thoroughfare beside it bears the delightful name of Holy Bones, for remains of sacrificed animals have been dug up there.

At the moment Leicester's buildings are passing through a transitional stage. Modern Leicester is largely brick-built, in the belief that the proper use of brick is more indicative of the modern

21   THE THREE SWANS INN,
MARKET HARBOROUGH, LEICESTERSHIRE

20   HOUSE IN HIGHCROSS STREET,
LEICESTER

22   THE OAK PARLOUR, QUENBY HALL,
LEICESTERSHIRE

23   THE TIMBERED INTERIOR, OLD TOWN HALL,
LEICESTER

spirit than glittering white stone. After sundry excursions into terra cotta combined with blue brick Leicester architects decided to stick to the principle that the less one attempts to do with brick the more effective will be the result. They will show you the Fire Station and the North Memorial Homes, but perhaps the finest specimen is the Crescent, in King Street; this was built after the style of the Bath show places, as private residences, but it is now mostly converted into offices.

[*Drawn by R. & J. A. Brandon*

ST. MARTIN'S CHURCH, LEICESTER: THE CHANCEL ROOF

Leicester claims that her two staple industries of hosiery and footwear manufacture are larger both in output and in the number of people they employ than in any other city in the world. The slogan "Leicester clothes the world" is meant to be taken literally. "Out of the rattle and clatter of the old stocking frame, a sound that was familiar enough in any street in Leicester a century ago, has grown the smooth incessant hum of an incredible variety of machines, all based on the simple device of the knitting needle, manufacturing every type of knitted garment conceivable. But

unfortunately for local pride Leicester cannot claim the invention
of the stocking frame. That distinction belongs to the Rev. William
Lee, of Calverton, near Nottingham, who with high hopes but
small reward introduced his machine to Queen Elizabeth in 1590."[1]

Leicester was, of course, the obvious centre for the establishment
of a hosiery industry, for the clay of the Soar Valley produced the
finest pastures in the world, and the town thrived on the wool they
yielded. The introduction of power looms in 1847 led to an in-
creasing mechanisation of the industry, and the gradual adaptation
of knitting machinery to meet a multitude of further uses. Leicester
made "cardigan" jackets for the troops in the Crimean War, and
now makes nearly everything else that people wear; its knitted
material for women's clothing is menacing the Yorkshire woollen
trade. Among satellite industries are spinning and dyeing, also
trimming and finishing, which must be carried out before the
clothes are ready to wear.

The making of boots and shoes is the younger of the city's two
big industries, for though they had been made there for centuries
it was not until 1850 when Thomas Crick discovered a method of
riveting soles to uppers instead of laboriously stitching them on with
waxed thread that the industry began to expand. The invention did
away with the old system of making boots to order and laid the
foundations of mass production, for the industry was able to supply
a much greater demand than that of Leicester alone. Following the
example of the hoisery manufacturers the boot and shoe industry
began to mechanise the manufacture of footwear as far as possible,
and it was not long after the appearance of Crick's invention that
the factory system for the making of boots and shoes was organised.
Previously it had been carried on in the workers' cottages, each
home being its own authority in the matter of hours and labour
conditions. American competition at the beginning of the present
century resulted in complete mechanisation so that now Leicester
is the largest footwear manufacturing centre in the world. Of her
250,000 population some 50,000 people are either employed in
making shoes or articles connected with shoe-making and in
distributing them.

I like Nottingham (18, 19)—I went courting there—and even in the
rain its Castle Rock gives me a thrill. But I must confess that its
people appear more aloof than those of Leicester; where Leicester
goes out of its way to help the stranger, Nottingham doesn't seem
to care a tinker's cuss what sort of difficulties you get into. Nottingham has not the wealth of ancient monuments possessed by Leicester
but it is more finely situated and its Castle Rock and riverside

[1] Courtesy of the Leicester Publicity and Development Bureau.

24, 25   LIVELINESS AT NOTTINGHAM GOOSE FAIR

26   LACE-CURTAIN MAKING AT A NOTTINGHAM FACTORY

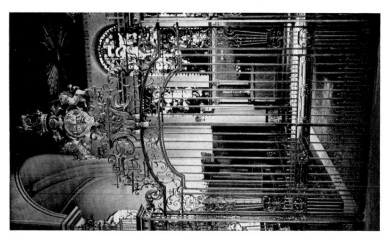

27 THE NORTH-EAST CORNER OF THE NAVE, INGESTRE CHURCH, STAFFORDSHIRE

28 THE EARLY EIGHTEENTH-CENTURY CHURCH AT MAPPLETON, DERBYSHIRE

29 THE CENTRAL GATES OF THE IRONWORK CHANCEL SCREEN, DERBY CATHEDRAL, DESIGNED

promenades are as good as anything any inland city in England can show. It is England's most inland river port, and historically is the more important of the two cities, but has been steadily overtaken by Leicester, whose position is more favourable in regard to transport and whose industries are not affected by depression. But the rivalry between the two towns is deep-seated. Nottingham saw the slow decay of her main industry, when lace went out of fashion, but I am told that it is coming back into favour again (26).

Nottingham's attraction lies more in what is new than in what is old. The Later Renaissance castle of 1674, burnt to a shell by the Reform Bill mobs of 1831, was in 1878 rehabilitated to form the art gallery and museum; the old gateway, dungeon, rock dwellings and dry moat remain to attract visitors. The city has some old inns; the Flying Horse, the Salutation Inn dating back to the fifteenth century, and the Trip to Jerusalem Inn, which opened its doors in 1189 and claims to have been a calling place for Crusaders on their way to the Holy Land. The rock cellars are believed to have been part of a Saxon cave settlement. Few of Nottingham's churches are old, but St. Peter's has some portions of the thirteenth century and St. Mary's of the fifteenth. Perhaps the town's finest possession is Wollaton Hall (107), a splendid house built in the time of Queen Elizabeth at a cost of £80,000; it is now the city's natural history museum. It is not the ordinary shape of an Elizabethan house, but is a square mansion of two storeys built round a central hall surmounted by a massive tower, with towers at each of the four corners. It belonged to the Willoughbys, of whom the most famous was the explorer Sir Hugh Willoughby whose ship became a frozen tomb off the ice-bound Lapland coast. The city also owns Newstead Abbey with its collection of Byron relics, but these must be described elsewhere. Nottingham's pride lies more in its fine new buildings; its Council House, Guildhall, War Memorial and University. It boasts of being the first town in England to maintain a university college out of the rates.

It is a curious fact that machinery was being used to make stockings more than three and a half centuries ago; before then they were made of cloth cut to shape and seamed at the back. I have already mentioned William Lee, the curate of Calverton, who produced the first machine for mechanical knitting. The frame which he invented was the forerunner of all present-day hosiery and lace machines. It was by a modification of the stocking frame between the years 1770 and 1800 that a lace mesh was first produced by mechanical means, and the improvements in the following century brought the manufacture of machine-made lace to its present high standard. The machinery for making lace is among the most wonderful machinery ever invented, and led to Nottingham and the

NMC : E

surrounding district becoming the largest lace-producing centre in the world. A visit to one of the factories is an eye-opener, but whether the industry will stage a come-back remains to be seen.

The jingling lines "The little smith of Nottingham, Who doth the work that no man can," indicate that the town was long famed for the skill of its iron-workers and engineers; now they make pretty nearly everything you can imagine, including such weird items as "bends, tees, collars, caps, plugs," whatever they may be. Brewing, tanning, tobacco, printing—but there's no end to the list; the name Byard Lane takes us back to the days when beer was sold by the yard. Fancy asking for eighteen inches of best bitter!

Derby is an old town, for the Roman station of Derventio stood here before the Saxons came. Later it was one of the five boroughs of the Danes which formed a federal commonwealth, each governed by its own laws. It numbered a hundred burgesses in Domesday Book. In 1745 Prince Charlie occupied the town and levied a contribution of £3000 on the inhabitants before he was reluctantly compelled to retreat northward. Yet for a town of such antiquity Derby is disappointing in its historical remains. Exeter House where the Young Pretender stayed is gone (though there is a Prince Charlie Room in the museum), as are the castle, city walls and gates—if it ever had any. An Elizabethan house known as the Mayor's Parlour was in danger of being pulled down when I was there, but the old chapel of Our Lady of the Brigg, on St. Mary's Bridge, has been carefully restored. A Jacobean House in the Wardwick, now used as a café, was partly dismantled in order to widen the street. There is the old Dolphin Inn, dating from 1530, but architecturally speaking there is hardly anything in the town worth looking at twice, with the exception of the cathedral. This was formerly the parish church and appears to have been made a cathedral against its wish. The only thing in the cathedral tradition is the embattled tower, which is good solid early sixteenth-century Perpendicular and one of the best in the Midlands (page 27). Otherwise it is just a quiet homely church with none of that high-pew feeling; actually the building was designed throughout by Gibbs, who has left on record his relief at being able to dispense with galleries. There are a few interesting monuments, including the tomb designed by herself of that celebrated Countess of Shrewsbury who was better known as "Bess of Hardwick"; but we shall hear enough about that formidable lady later. Perhaps the finest thing in the church is the great Cavendish screen and altar rail, whose delicate scrolls and foliage make it a magnificent example of Robert Bakewell's ironwork (29). The screen, font-cover and gate in St. Werburgh's Church are also his work, as are the iron gates of the old Derwent Silk Mill now outside the museum. It was at St. Werburgh's that Dr. Johnson married his beloved "Tetty" on July 9th, 1735. The Roman Catholic Church of St. Mary's, built in 1838, is said to be one of Pugin's best designs. If you are a follower of Herbert Spencer you will find his house, marked by a tablet, in Exeter Street.

Derby is the home of transport. First the railway and then the motor-car helped put the town on the industrial map of England, for at the L.M.S. works they produce all kinds of railway engines and rolling stock, and at the Rolls-Royce plant the finest cars in the world are made, and now also aero-engines and dynamos. But it was for textiles, not machinery, that Derby was originally famous, for it was in 1717 that the first silk mill in England was opened there by John Lombe. He gained the secret of spinning or "throwing" silk after visiting Italy in disguise and bribing some of the workmen, some of whom he brought back with him. He died soon after the mill was built, poisoned, so the story goes, by an Italian woman employed by the manufacturers whose secret he had stolen. The silk factory has long been closed, and the town is now better known for the Crown Derby Porcelain Works, which has held an unrivalled position in the ceramic world since the manufacture of china was begun in 1750.

Did you know that Derby is the "Stoniton" of *Adam Bede*?

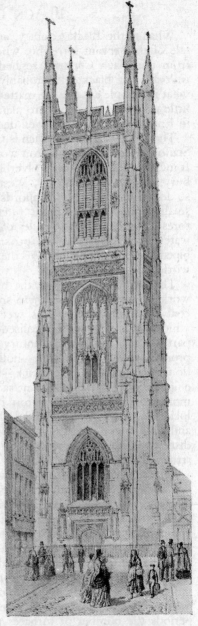

[*Drawn by Charles Wickes, 1854*]

THE TOWER, ALL SAINTS, DERBY
(now the cathedral)

BLACK COUNTRY

What is the Black Country, and how did it get its name? The tale of the servant girl who, when told that a friend of hers came from the Black Country, replied: "Where on earth is that? She isn't all that black," is probably apocryphal, but where it is and what its people are like are matters of which the "foreigner" knows little or nothing. There are plenty of other dirty, squalid districts in England which might well dispute the title.

The "Black Country" then is that unlovely area of south-western Staffordshire where the iron-working trades are carried on (12). It includes the towns of Wolverhampton, Dudley, Walsall, Wednesbury, Tipton, Bilston (30), West Bromwich and Smethwick, and so does not lie wholly in Staffordshire. Actually it is a comparatively small area, covering about fifteen miles by ten. Here beautiful forests have changed to miles of furnaces, slag-heaps and stagnant water pools, for the close proximity of iron, coal and clay combined to make this one of the greatest industrial areas in the world.

The Black Country was the historic centre of England's metal-working industries, and these smoky towns which rise above the coal measures each had its specialised products. A list showing which industries where localised in certain areas during the latter part of the nineteenth century gives the following towns and products: West Bromwich—hollow-ware, safes, springs, constructional engineering; Smethwick—screws, sheet glass, constructional engineering; Walsall—leather, saddlery and harness, saddlers' ironmongery, locks, brushes, iron tubes; Wednesbury—tubes, gun-locks; Darlaston—nuts and bolts, gun-locks; Willenhall—locks and keys, curry-combs; Wednesfield—locks and keys; Dudley and district—wrought nails, chain and anchor, fenders, fire-irons, constructional engineering.

Here the wealth of England was born, but the towns grew too fast for proper planning and were literally thrown together. Yet the folk who live here appear to accept their industry-scarred landscape with equanimity, though not without giving derisive nicknames to some of its worst features. Names such as Hell Hole, Hell Lane, Quality Square, Ragman's Row and Bugs' Gutter abound, and Graveyard and Paradise are met with, though the latter is far from being a heavenly resort.

People who lived in this smoke-bound wilderness say it isn't nearly so black as it was fifty years ago, for except during boom periods the number of furnaces producing finished iron has been steadily decreasing since the Franco-German war of 1870. The development of lighter forms of industry and improvements in housing conditions have awakened public conscience, and pit-mounds and slag-heaps are being planted with trees and shrubs and made into gardens; now it is suggested that the designation "grey" ought to be substituted for "Black."

For four hundred years the Black Country has been a famous iron-working centre, though documentary evidence proves that the trade was carried on as early as the thirteenth century. Until the middle of the eighteenth century charcoal was used for smelting, and though Dud Dudley experimented with coal smelting in 1619 his method was not generally accepted. Nowadays most of the iron comes from Spain (though I have helped bring it by ship from beyond North Cape). A blast-furnace is an awesome sight. It is a huge round tower seventy or a hundred feet high, and by the light of its furious red glow the men handling the molten metal appear like gnomes engaged in some monstrous underworld activity. That local people are not insensible to this rather unearthly atmosphere is shown in the couplet:

> When Satan stood on Brierley Hill and far around he gazed,
> He said: "I never more shall feel at hell's fierce flames amazed."

The devil is said to have lain down to die near Dudley, in despair, for the fires he saw there made a better hell than the one he ruled. Now Brierley Hill is better known for its bacon factory, the largest in England.

Black Country people are like their landscape, unbeautiful, unsentimental, with no time for the trimmings of life, but often a warm, if rough, hospitality hides behind the forbidding exterior. Black Country speech is hard for an outsider to understand. It contains inflexions no longer used in everyday English. *I bin, thee bist, we bist, yo bin, they bin* are declensions of the verb *to be*. *Will* becomes *woon* or *woot* and *a* is often sounded as *o*. Can you translate these? "We dey arf goo acoming back in that theer chara." "Poor owd Alf's jed, let's 'ope 'e's gone weer we think 'e ain't." Black Country humour is also characteristic. "What are you looking for, Ned?" a collier was asked by his friends. "I've lost me weskit," Ned replied. "Why, y' foo' y' gotten it on!" "Ah, so I have," exclaimed Ned. "Now if you hadn't told me I should have gone whum without it." Then there is the story of the man at Darlaston who used to shut the toll-gate to keep out the bad weather. Another man tried to entice the weather-cock off the steeple with dried peas. These stories are akin to those concerning the villagers of Gotham, in Nottinghamshire, who built a hedge to keep the cuckoo from flying away.

I have been told that dog-fights are still organised in this district, though I have been unable to verify the fact. "It's a better sport than football or gee-gees," my informant told me. Dog-fighting used to be a popular pastime in the Black Country and Staffordshire bull-terriers were bred and trained for the sport. Fights used to be staged in secret, on old pit-mounds or ruined buildings, and men were posted as look-outs to watch for the approach of the police. A fight would last until one of the dogs was killed, and often considerable sums of money were won or lost. But naturally no strangers are allowed to attend these meetings.

Though the towns of the Black Country are usually regarded just as dingy industrial centres, many of them are ancient and interesting. Wolverhampton's name is a corruption of Wulfruna's town, for the sister of King Edgar founded a Saxon college here in 996. Now it is a great town of more than 100,000 people with a large old parish church in the Perpendicular style; it has several old monuments, among them a twelve-foot Norman cross usually known as the "Dane's Cross." Wolverhampton also used to have—and may still have—a funny old inn known as the Upside Down House, with rooms tilted at curious angles, so that the landlord delighted in showing visitors how a bottle could apparently roll uphill. Walsall is another ancient town, but apart from the curious custom of throwing apples and nuts from the town hall on St. Clement's day, "to be scrambled for by the populace," it has little of interest, beyond its making of horse brasses.

The town of Dudley is an isolated piece of Worcestershire surrounded by Staffordshire territory, but Dudley Castle on its hill belongs to Staffordshire. The frowning walls and towers and ruined keep stand on the foundations of the eighth-century fortress erected by the Saxon prince Dud. It was besieged for three weeks during the Civil War, and after being damaged by fire in 1750 was never rebuilt. The hill is a mass of Silurian limestone pushed up from the surrounding coalfields, and its interior is a maze of chambers, galleries and shafts where the quarrymen have been at work. Four miles away is Holbeach House, near Himley, on the site of the old mansion where the Gunpowder Plot conspirators were captured after a bloody fight.

Wednesbury is also a place of great antiquity for a castle was built there in the tenth century by Ethelfleda, the daughter of King Alfred. The town itself is still older for its Saxon name was Wodensburgh. Wednesbury was considered to be the capital of the Black Country, and what life was like there a hundred years ago can be gleaned from a poem by Amy Lyons in *Black Country Sketches*.

> In Wednesbury town, a town whose name
> Is coupled with its cocking fame,
> Was yearly held by custom's right,
> A wake where colliers met to fight,

Where bulls were baited, torn, abused,
And dogs were killed, which much amused
These sturdy knights of coal and hammer
Who scoff at peace and joy at clamour.

POTTERY TOWNS

The famous "Five Towns" of Arnold Bennett really consist of
six towns: Burslem, Fenton, Hanley, Longton, Stoke and Tunstall,
which in 1910 amalgamated to form one big town called Stoke-on-
Trent. It was the largest experiment in local government that had
taken place, but the result has best been summed up by J. B.
Priestley in his *English Journey*: "This city has a population of nearly
300,000, but it has no real existence as a city of that size. There is
no city. There are still those six little towns. After federation into
one city had been first suggested, the inhabitants of those towns
argued and quarrelled most bitterly for years. Finally the obvious
advantages of federation carried the day, and there appeared, on
paper, the mythical city of Stoke-on-Trent. But when you go
there, you still see the six towns, looking like six separate towns.
Unless you are wiser than I was, you will never be quite certain
which of the six you are in at any given time, but at least you will
be ready to swear that you are nowhere near a city that contains
300,000 people." The old market town of Newcastle-under-Lyme
adjoins, but is not part of, the Potteries, as it is careful to point out.

The Potteries is a curiously self-contained area, perhaps ten miles
long by three or four miles wide, straggling along the valleys that
form the headwaters of the Trent. It is a hilly district and east and
west the high moors hem it in closely. Factories crowd the valleys
and not a yard of space is left uncovered. It is so densely populated
that all signs of Nature's handiwork appear to have been obliterated.
Because its natural conditions have thus kept it within rigid bounds
the factory area does not sprawl over the surrounding countryside
in patchy settlements, half residential, half industrial; where the
Potteries stop the real country begins. Pleasant scenery is never
very far away.

Judged by most standards it is an ugly district. The industry is
carried on in a great number of small-scale units and so lacks the
impressiveness of huge, if dingy, cotton mills and shipyards.
This is a landscape painted in the red and grey of "pot-banks" and
coal-pits and steel-work. Everywhere there are chimneys and
narrow-necked kilns like huge dirty milk bottles, and slimy canals
and rubbish tips. This scenery is repeated over and over till it
becomes wearisome. The architecture of the various towns has been
described as an outrage, but it is no worse than the usual squalor

and dreariness of English nineteenth-century towns, the common
stuff of which most of our big industrial cities was made. They are
timeless towns of no history. Yet here, as elsewhere, one is struck by
the attachment which people form for their mean and smoky habita-
tion. It seems a pity that people whose skill maintains a traditional
craft in modern dress could not have better towns to live in.

Stoke may be said to have literally grown up round the pottery
works started by Josiah Wedgwood in the latter half of the eighteenth
century. But even earlier rough pottery had been made at Burslem
(31) and in 1626 a monopoly was granted to Thomas Ram and
Abraham Cullen "for the sole making of the Stone Potte, Stone
Jugge, and Stone Bottle within our Dominions, for a term of
Fowerteene yeares." A little later two Dutch brothers named Elers
developed the smooth red earthenware and salt-glaze pottery. The
story goes that they kept their process secret by employing only
half-witted workers, but when some of these developed sufficient
wit to pass on the knowledge to other potters then the Dutchmen
decided it was time to move to London. The great Josiah began
his first pottery in a small house called Ivy Cottage and prospered
sufficiently to build at Etruria the historic factory which paved the
way for the huge industry carried on in the "Five Towns." Wedgwood's genius lay in his love of experiment, and the beautiful
pottery produced at Etruria became world-famous. "Wedgwood"
ware, "Majolica," "Queen's" and "Rockingham" ware and
Parian statuary were among the finest examples of ceramic art.
By the end of the century imitation Delft ware had superseded the
Dutch original . As the industry expanded it was found necessary
to import clay from Devon and Dorset, which was brought by sea
to Runcorn on the Mersey and then by canals to the Potteries.
Wedgwood's work was greatly helped by the invention of transfer
printing between 1750 and 1760 by John Sadler of Liverpool.

There are several monuments to Wedgwood in and about Stoke,
but probably he would consider Etruria his best memorial. And
though Pottery folk can tell you all about him and his family (32),
one person they don't seem to know very much about is Arnold
Bennett.

SALT TOWNS

There are other industrial areas of the North Midlands, of lesser
importance and interest, too many to describe in detail here. The
district along the Derbyshire-Nottinghamshire border, from Dronfield to Long Eaton, is gradually becoming a network of collieries,
mills and factories. D. H. Lawrence described this region in several
books, among them *Sons and Lovers*. Coalfields also make unlovely
far too much of the beautiful scenery of Charnwood Forest in

30 CANALSIDE WORKS, NEAR BILSTON, STAFFORDSHIRE

31 THE CANAL AT BURSLEM, STAFFORDSHIRE

[From a painting by George Stubbs

32   THE WEDGWOOD FAMILY

[From an engraving by Michael Burghers
for Plot's "History of Staffordshire"

33‾ MADELEY MANOR, STAFFORDSHIRE

Leicestershire, while Cannock Chase in Staffordshire is succumbing to the same complaint. Surface ironstone working is extending among the Wolds bordering the Vale of Belvoir (17), though I am told the land reverts to farming afterwards; I hope this is true.

I will finish with a few words about the Salt Towns of Cheshire, which must surely be among the queerest of all our English towns. The Salt Field occupies the central portion of the county, along the River Weaver, where agriculture suddenly gives place to a vigorous industrial development. Northwich, Middlewich, and Winsford are built over the salt workings, and smoking chimneys, rows of dilapidated buildings, lines of pumps and steam pipes demonstrate that the ancient Cheshire salt industry is still flourishing. It is hard to realise that Northwich has a history reaching back to Roman times; *Salinae* it was called in those days. Many of the houses are screwed and bolted together to keep them secure, but old inhabitants prophesy that if the salt works keep on long enough a great portion of the area will be buried under water.

Northwich is one of the busiest and dirtiest towns in England, both of which distinctions it possesses because it is the principal centre of the salt trade. Although a place of considerable antiquity there is little of interest to see there, for the whole neighbourhood bears that atmosphere of desolation and untidiness common to mining areas. But its Salt Museum is unique, with its crystals, old tools, and curious things found in the salt. The only other "sight" is underground. This is Marston Old Mine, a vast subterranean hall whose roof is supported by massive pillars of crystal and which, when lit up by lamps and candles, resembles a veritable fairyland. On State occasions it is opened up for the delectation of royal visitors, and some—the Tsar of Russia among them—have dined and wined in its glittering hall. Rock salt was discovered here by accident in 1670, when drilling for coal; the place was worked for over a hundred years and covers thirty-five acres. Now mining for salt has been abandoned except in one 300-foot mine.

Camden wrote of Northwich that "it was in British Hellath du, signifying the black salt-pit, where there is a deep and plentiful brine-pit, with stairs about it, by which, when they have drawn the water in their leather buckets, they ascend half naked to the troughs and fill them; from whence it is conveyed to the Wich Houses, that are furnished with great piles of wood." The more modern method is to pump the brine out of the earth into a reservoir, from where it is conveyed by pipes into salt-pans, which are wide shallow vessels of iron covered with wooden roofs, with furnaces underneath to heat the brine and cause it to evaporate into coarse white salt.

III

NORTH MIDLAND COUNTRYSIDE
HIGH PEAK TO SHERWOOD

A LITTLE girl evacuated to a certain Derbyshire village was overheard to remark in her prayers: "Lead us not into temptation but deliver us from Edale, Amen!" Ramblers who have been marooned there for the night have been heard to express a similar prayer, though couched in more forcible terms. For Edale is in the very heart of the Peak, a secluded little place of a few houses, a church and an inn; it is the centre from which the area can best be explored.

Now the odd thing about the Peak District is that it does not possess a peak worthy of the name. "But where is *the* peak?" is a question often asked by strangers in Derbyshire, and reluctantly the answer comes: "There isn't one." Visitors who look in vain for a single dominating summit must blame Dr. Johnson for defining a peak as a "sharply pointed hill"; actually it is doubtful if the word ever meant this, Pecseatas being the name given to the first Saxon settlers, hence Peac-land.

Now the term Peak District is loosely applied to the hilly district of north-west Derbyshire and such parts of adjacent counties as physically belong to it (34). Geologically it is a flat-topped plateau of millstone grit, adjoining a lower plateau of carboniferous limestone. There is no High Peak proper, no isolated summit; the highest elevation is the so-called Kinderscout plateau above Edale. So unpeaklike is this flat boggy stretch of elevated moorland, with an average height of just over 2000 feet, that it does not even possess a name. Or rather it had many names, for the people in the various neighbouring valleys called it by different titles. This sprawling mountain mass is the nearest thing to a real High Peak, so the name has very improperly been attached to it.

Gritstone scenery is grim, something like the Scottish highlands in miniature, all bogs and heather and black rock, and peaty streams running down through hidden valleys known as "cloughs." The

34

[*From an engraving by J. Greig*

34   PEVERIL CASTLE, THE PEAK, DERBYSHIRE

[*After a drawing by E. Dayes*

35   THE PEAK CAVERN, DERBYSHIRE

36 DERBYSHIRE UPLANDS ABOVE DOVEDALE

37 A QUIET STRETCH IN THE PEAK DISTRICT
NEAR MIDDLETON, DERBYSHIRE

"tops," as the high moors are called, are not crossed by a single road, save where the highway from Glossop to Sheffield cuts diagonally across to the Derwent Valley. There are few footpaths, for practically the whole of the district is private property, and rights of way are scarce. The land belongs either to municipal waterworks or to sporting interests. The former refuse access to the public on the pretext that the water might become polluted, the latter rent the land as grouse moors and maintain an army of gamekeepers to see that outsiders do not venture off a few well-defined routes. Thus some forty miles of country is all but closed to walkers, a situation resembling that in the Scottish Highlands, where deer count for more than men; here grouse come first. This is not to say that people accept this state of affairs with equanimity; every now and again a mass-trespass takes place and fines and imprisonment result, while there is a never-ending battle between keepers and individual trespassers. Indeed, the sport of "dodging the keeper" is popular amongst the more adventurous ramblers.

But it should not be forgotten that what few rights of access the public does possess were won only after an untiring fight by the Peak District and Northern Counties Footpaths Preservation Society, and a lot of heated controversy was necessary before notice-boards such as the following made their appearance on these hitherto inviolable moors: "F. J. Sumner, Esq., and others have conceded permission and right for the public in perpetuity to traverse on foot this moorland by the route indicated by posts, on the understanding that this is the route to be followed and that there be no divergence therefrom or trespass upon any parts of the moor." Such is freedom in England!

The classic ramble in the Peak is the twenty-one-mile circuit of Kinderscout, by public footpath. Stand by the Church Hotel in Edale and see the ramblers go stamping off with their hobnailed boots and bulging rucksacks—"filled with nothing but their tea and the determination to take the first bus home" as somebody unkindly remarked to me once—and you will hear all sorts of curious and intriguing names mentioned: Mount Famine, Ringing Roger, Red Brook, Jacob's Ladder, Shining Tor, and a place with the ominous name of Featherbed Moss. A fine sight in wet weather is Kinder Downfall plunging over its precipice; it is Derbyshire's only real waterfall. Near the Downfall is the Mermaid's Pool, with the usual legend. In this locality Mrs. Humphrey Ward laid the early scenes of her novel *David Grieve*. The top of Kinder is forbidden ground (those who have trespassed there say it isn't worth it, being only several square miles of peaty wilderness), but the path up William Clough is wild enough for most ramblers. Here at 1700 feet the forbidding heights sweep away in a vast

semi-circle, all purple, green and gold, and out of the black bogs
rise splintered gritstone tors through which the wind howls dis-
mally. It is landscape reduced to elemental terms. Beyond lies the
Snake Inn with the cup—or is it glass?—that cheers.

South of the Vale of Edale is the Hope Valley, in which lies
Castleton, famous for its caverns. This is one of the loveliest
pastoral valleys in Derbyshire, and is the dividing line between the
gritstone masses to the north and the limestone uplands to the
south. Derbyshire has four distinct types of scenery, based on four
main geological divisions. The gritstone region of the High Peak
occupies the north-western corner, while immediately south is the
limestone country of the Low Peak. The heathery moors and bogs
of the gritstone contrast sharply with the rolling grassy uplands and
white-walled dales of the limestone; the abrupt change is very
striking. In turn, the limestone gives way to sandstone, which
stretches to the Trent and beyond, producing typical Midland
landscape of half-timbered houses, cornfields and woodlands. East
of the Derwent are coalfields and all that they imply. Here and
there, as at Matlock and Miller's Dale, are masses of volcanic rock
known as toadstone.

The characteristic view of Castleton shows a compact, stone-
built village nestling beneath a precipitous hill, dominated by the
square keep of Peak Castle (34). Seen from a distance the castle
appears quite romantic, but visitors who succumb to its lure and
toil heroically up the steep hillside find that it consists of little more
than a ruined wall and gateway and the roofless shell of the keep.
Sir Walter Scott's *Peveril of the Peak* is responsible for the pseudo-
glamour attaching to the place, though the existence of anyone
bearing that name in the seventeenth century is pure fiction. The
Peveril who built the original stronghold in 1068 was the Conqueror's
illegitimate son; it was the seat of government in the High Peak in
Norman times. Here Henry II, a century later, received the sub-
mission of Malcolm, King of Scotland, and celebrated the event by
consuming wine to the value of seventy-two Plantagenet shillings.
One of the Earls of Derby once stormed and captured the place;
those who have climbed the hill will appreciate the feat.

Beside the village green the fifteenth-century tower of the church
rises above the sycamores. It contains a beautiful Norman chancel
arch dating from the days of the Peverils, an old octagonal font,
and some seventeenth-century box pews of carved oak. The
library in the vestry, consisting of a thousand or so volumes, contains a "Breeches Bible" of 1611 and a Cranmer's Bible of 1539.
Castleton was a place where old customs lingered; the curfew used
to be rung every evening from the 29th of September until Shrove
Tuesday. Another interesting local custom takes place on the 29th

of May, or Oakapple Day; this being the Garland Festival. A man is chosen to be king of the festivities; he rides round town on horseback, wearing a large, bell-shaped garland of wild flowers. Beside him rides his queen, a youth dressed in a lady's riding habit and veil, while escorting them are Morris dancers and a brass band. They all march to the church, where the garland is hoisted to one of the pinnacles of the tower by the bellringers.

But Castleton's main claim to fame rests on its caverns, of which Peak and Speedwell Caverns and Blue John Mine are the most accessible. They can all be comfortably explored, with guides, for a moderate sum. Peak Cavern (35) is perhaps the most widely known. It is entered through a great natural arch known as the Devil's Hole (once used as a workshop by local ropemakers), and leads for nearly half a mile through a series of chambers and galleries, complete with the usual underground river, to all of which appropriate fanciful names have been given. You get good value for your money. "If due notice be given a choir of singers may be stationed to add to the effect," an old edition of Murray's *Guide* informs us, but in these enlightened days there seems to be no demand for their services. Speedwell Cavern is partly artificial, for it is reached by a disused mine shaft sunk over a hundred years ago by a party of disillusioned prospectors. It contains a real wonder, a cave known as the Great Hall whose ceiling is so lofty that rockets have reached a height of 450 feet without touching the roof. There is also a Bottomless Pit ninety feet deep. Blue John Mine extends for three miles into the heart of a hollow hill. The famous Blue John spar is obtained here; it is made into vases and ornaments, and two vases made of it were dug up at Pompeii.

Mention of caves brings us to the oft-discussed Seven Wonders of the Peak, though visitors should be warned that they may not come up to expectation, the standard in wonders having risen considerably since Charles Cotton rhapsodised about them in mediocre verse. But Peak Cavern and Chatsworth House (54) are definitely up to wonder-standard, while Mam Tor and Eldon Hole are worth honourable mention. The former is a 1700-foot summit with a crumbling sandstone face which has given it the name of Shivering Mountain; the latter is an awesome chasm in a hillside, which drops 265 feet into unseen depths. The story of the goose which was seen to fly down Eldon Hole and emerge from Peak Cavern without a single feather on its back is just another of those local legends, I fear. Why the romantic gorge of the Winnats (or Wind Gates) near by, with its fantastic limestone cliffs and its tale of murdered lovers, was not included in the list of wonders, it is difficult to say. Of the remaining Peakland wonders, the ebbing and flowing well at Tideswell no longer ebbs and flows (another ebbing and flowing

well near Sparrowpit contests Tideswell's claim to the title; though
you may have to wait a long time to see it work), Poole's Hole near
Buxton comes a poor second to the Castleton caves, while St. Anne's
well, also at Buxton, is quite a profitable wonder, judged as a
commercial proposition.

The old church at Hope, a mile or so down the valley, was
restored in the fourteenth century and restored again some 500 years
later in much worse taste. The best of the old-time work is gone,
though the fifteenth century is represented by some truly awful
gargoyles. Instead of a statue of St. Peter in the niche over the
porch they formerly hung dead foxes there so as to be able to
claim the money offered for the destruction of such vermin. There
is a Jacobean pulpit of carved oak, and some old chairs, one of
which was the schoolmaster's throne when the village school was
held in the church. A quaint little brass depicts one of the Balguys,
who procured a weekly market and four fairs for Hope. The
seven-foot shaft of a Saxon cross, decorated with the conventional
knotwork and foliage, stands in the churchyard, near some engraved
coffin stones of the thirteenth century. Roman work can be found
a mile away at Brough, where the camp known as Anavio dates
from the second century; but there is little to be seen now.

South of the Vale of Hope the rolling limestone uplands of
Bradwell and Abney Moors stretch away to Buxton and the Wye
Valley. This is a bright and smiling land of close-cropped turf,
and old forgotten green roads where you can tramp tirelessly mile
after mile, wonderful walking after the weary footslogging over
the gritstone "tops." How different too from the gritstone, for
here are no keepers or "Trespassers will be prosecuted" signs;
though Heaven help you if you are caught bathing in the strictly
preserved trout streams! It is lovable country, and a thirsty country,
too, on a hot summer's day, for the rivers all run underground.
Characteristic are the drystone walls which stretch for miles, for
though the name of moor clings to these uplands they were public
commons until enclosed a century and a half ago. The Saxons
farmed this land, and the district has more names in Domesday Book
than any other part of the north. The moors are pitted with the
shafts of old lead mines, and prehistoric burial mounds and stone
circles crown the gentle summits. In remote stone-built villages
and lonely farms the people cling to old beliefs and customs found
nowhere else in Britain. Peak Forest, for example, was a local
Gretna Green; of this forest, as an old writer puts it: "Trees I doe
acknowledge are so few, that had Judas been there, he would have
repented, before he could have found one to act his execution."

In this area are two villages which vie with each other in visitor-
appeal, Tideswell (38) and Eyam. Eyam, of course, is known far

38   TIDESWELL VILLAGE, DERBYSHIRE

39   WELL-DRESSING AT TISSINGTON, DERBYSHIRE

40 TIDESWELL CHURCH, DERBYSHIRE

41 NORBURY CHURCH, DERBYSHIRE
BOTH OF THE DECORATED STYLE (FOURTEENTH CENTURY)

and wide as the Plague Village. Most people probably know the
story, but it may be new to some. When the great plague of 1665
attacked the village, carried there in a box of clothing ordered by
the tailor from London, the vicar, William Mompesson, elected to
stay with his stricken parishioners rather than to seek safety elsewhere. To prevent the plague spreading nobody was allowed to
leave the village; the people of Eyam remained completely isolated
for over a year. Mompesson and his wife cared for the sick, main-
tained order, and held daily services in a small glen known as
Cucklet Delf. In these tasks they were assisted by Thomas Stanley,
the former rector, who had been ejected from the church for Nonconformity, but who still resided in the village. Meanwhile whole
families were dying off, and soon there were not enough people
left to bury the dead. At long last, after thirteen months of suffering,
the plague died away; out of some 350 inhabitants only ninety were
left. Mompesson's wife was among those who had died. Shortly
afterwards he moved to the living at Eakring, in Nottinghamshire,
but the people refused to have him for fear he carried the plague,
and for a time he was forced to live in a hut in the woods. But he
lived long enough to become a Prebend of York and Southwell.
As for Stanley, his loving congregation showed their gratitude for
what he had done by trying to turn him out of the village because
of his Nonconformity, and only the intervention of the Earl of
Devonshire saved him.

Eyam still possesses memorials of this tragic event, though the
so-called Plague Cottages pointed out to visitors are probably not
the originals, which were most likely destroyed for fear of harbour-
ing infection. Food had been left at the village boundary, and
payment for it deposited in a trough of running water; Mompesson's
Well, as it was called, can still be seen. At Cucklet Delf, the open-
air church, a procession and a service takes place every August to
honour the two brave men. The Riley Graves, in a near-by field,
mark the resting place of the Hancock family, seven of whom died
in eight days, leaving only the mother to bury them. Stanley and
Mompesson have a brass memorial inside the church, and in the
chancel is a carved oak chair with the legend "Mom. 1665. Eyam,"
recovered from a second-hand shop in Liverpool. An old oak
cupboard in the vestry is said to have come from one of the Plague
Cottages. This vestry was once the retreat of a gay-hearted vicar
named Joseph Hunt, who having got drunk at the local inn, went
through a form of marriage with the landlord's daughter. He then
discovered that the tie was binding, and as he happened to be
engaged to a girl in Derby who promptly sued him for breach of
promise, found himself faced with a bill for damages which he
could not pay. So to avoid arrest he shut himself up in the vestry.

His parishioners were a sporting crowd, for they brought him food and kept a look-out for the police. Afterwards—but unfortunately history becomes silent at this point.

Tideswell (38), 900 feet up on the edge of bleak uplands, has not the sadness which pervades Eyam. It is a curious mixture of ancient and modern, but the pride of its heart is the splendid Decorated church (40), which old writers loved to call the "Cathedral of the Peak." Cruciform in shape, and dating mainly from the middle of the fourteenth century, the finest part of the church is probably the chancel, often described as "one gallery of light and beauty."

And so to Buxton. Spa-fiends can talk glibly of thermal and chalybeate waters, and quote distinguished visitors' remarks, from Mary Queen of Scots' farewell lament to Macaulay's caustic comment that formerly visitors were regaled with oatcakes and a viand which the hosts called mutton but which the guests strongly suspected to be dog. And though I reap a whirlwind I must express doubts that Buxton ever was a popular Roman bathing-resort, since, apart from soldiers stationed at the forts along the Roman road, there were probably very few Romans in this wild hill country. Claiming to be the highest market town in England, a thousand feet or so above sea level, Buxton's streets, buildings, walks and gardens have all the spaciousness of the eighteenth-century spa. With nothing spectacular in the way of architecture (its oldest chapel dates only from 1625), it yet possesses a certain charm, its builders having avoided the folly of using anything except local materials. "Nobody, or scarcely anybody, has committed the crime of building a brick house in Buxton; even the multiple stores have been shamed into a certain reticence; while the railway station is an admirable symmetrical composition." Its chief architectural glory is the Crescent (43), a handsome range of buildings, including an assembly room, public and private baths, and a couple of hotels. It was designed in the Doric style by John Carr of York in 1780, to rival James Wood's Crescent at Bath, and cost the fifth Duke of Devonshire £120,000. Proud Buxtonians also point to the Pump Room, and the Devonshire Hospital, whose huge dome is said to be the largest in Europe. Opposite it is St. John's Church, an early nineteenth-century structure whose imposing portico and cupola are the work of Sir Jeffrey Wyatville, architect to the sixth Duke of Devonshire But probably the finest thing in Buxton is the Duke's Drive out of it.

South of Buxton lies Axe Edge, a bulky gritstone mass whose 1800 feet of heather, moss and wimberry constitutes the last really high summit of the Pennines. Axe Edge might well be called the "Head of Rivers," for it is the source of five celebrated streams. The Goyt and the Dane flow westward to the Cheshire Plain, the

42 NEW MILLS, DERBYSHIRE

43 THE CRESCENT, BUXTON, DERBYSHIRE
DESIGNED BY JOHN CARR OF YORK, 1780

44 MILLDALE, DOVEDALE, DERBYSHIRE

45 THE IRON TORS, DOVEDALE, DERBYSHIRE

Dove (45) and the Manifold (46) flow south through wonderful limestone valleys to join the Trent, the Wye flows eastward to join the Derwent. The chief joy of the Peak District is its rivers (6), and it is doubtful if any other region can show such a group of glorious streams, each in its individual way a scenic gem. This is the country of the dales, those steep-walled valleys which open suddenly in the rolling limestone uplands disclosing vistas of old stone farmhouses, green meadows, and hanging woodlands far below. The Dales vie with each other in beauty and historic interest, but we cannot within the space of this book visit them all; the Wye must serve as a type. The usual exit from Buxton is by the road which follows the Wye through a series of winding dales to Bakewell. This is typical romantic limestone scenery, though Ashwood Dale with its Lover's Leap is marred somewhat by a sewage works, and Ashford Dale by quarrying, while Miller's Dale, also, is selling its scenic birthright for hard cash. (Or, for the real enjoyment of beauty, is it best *not* to see certain things?) But nothing can equal the magnificent horsehoe of Chee Dale, with the sheer cliffs of Chee Tor towering 300 feet above the stream (14), or Monsal Dale (13) with its wealth of woodlands and rocky gorges. No road penetrates this wonderland, and though the railway follows the river it does so at a discreet distance. This is the same railway of which Ruskin wrote "this valley is now desecrated in order that a Buxton fool may be able to find himself in Bakewell at the end of twelve minutes." But it must be admitted that a railway need not necessarily spoil a landscape. We are apt to assume that reservoirs, quarries, mills and mines are not natural to the scenery of a place and spoil the look of it, but actually they are just as much a part of the scenery as churches, manors and cottages. For what we think of as natural to a scene, the houses, fields and woodlands, are not natural at all, but the hard-won results of many generations of careful workmanship. England in its natural state would be largely swamp and wilderness. The only reason for the villages, fields and woodlands being there is the same reason for the mills and quarries being there, that is, utility. The real cause of complaint is that industrial undertakings are so often erected without any attempt to harmonise with the scenery (cheapness and easy exploitation being the guiding principles) that we have come to consider industry as synonymous with ugliness. But this need not be so.

Finest of all the valleys is Dovedale (45), about which so much has already been written. A lengthy description of its beauties would be futile; all I can say is, go and see it. The best of it is the seven miles between Hartington and Thorpe Cloud, following the path downstream—there is no road. Beresford Dale is a little gem, with the tall pinnacle of Pike Rock rising out of its dark pool, but

NMC : G

the glory of the Dove is the tall white cliffs rising above the wood-lands. These have been carved into all sorts of weird, intriguing formations, to which the usual fanciful names have been attached (the natural bridge leading to Reynard's Cave always fascinates me). But candidly, I must confess I like my scenic features to have a name, and I suspect that many other people share my weakness. It is difficult to appraise scenery for lack of technical terms, but one can say of Dovedale that there is just the right combination of rock, timber and water, the scenic ingredients are just as they should be. Without having seen Cheddar Gorge I doubt if it can equal Dove-dale, though Dr. Johnson's remark that he who has seen Dovedale has no need to visit the Highlands is just foolishness. You cannot compare Japanese prints with Flemish old masters. Almost as fascinating as the Dove is its kindred river the Manifold (48); the two rise within half a mile of each other and are rarely more than a couple of miles apart. The Manifold comes plunging down through rocky hills where the Peak District overflows into Stafford-shire. The view of Thor's Cave hill (46) rising above the dark woodlands along the river is one of the finest things I know. All this country is saturated with the personalities of those two men, Charles Cotton and Izaak Walton, whose exploits are commemor-ated in *The Compleat Angler*. The famous Fishing House (61) which they built in 1674 still stands, also the packhorse bridge which Cotton so humorously described, and the cave in which he hid from his creditors. It is good to know that the light railway track along the Manifold has been converted into a public footpath.

Dovedale and Kinderscout are the two areas in the Peak which have been suggested as suitable for National Parks. What are National Parks, some may ask? Well, first clear your mind of the typical English conception of a park. National Parks may be defined as tracts of country (say 200 square miles), of especial beauty or wildness, preserved in their natural state and protected from spolia-tion by industry or "development," to which people have complete freedom of access, where they may camp, put up at a hostel, climb, swim or ramble, and generally enjoy a healthy out-of-doors holiday. The more organised our population becomes the more necessary it is for them to have access to breathing-spaces in the country to which they can retreat from time to time. Such breathing-spaces are a vital need, for there is something in the spirit of man which will not let him rest in his great cities, but is always calling him back to the soil from which his fathers came. "I demand that there be left waste spaces and wilds," wrote William Morris, "or romance and poetry, that is Art, will die out amongst us." And it is signi-ficant that Viscount Samuel in his book *An Unknown Land* makes the people of that modern Utopia resort every so often to log cabins

47 DEWPOND AND THOR'S CAVE,
NEAR WETTON, STAFFORDSHIRE

46 THOR'S CAVE, MANIFOLD VALLEY,
STAFFORDSHIRE

49 KINVER EDGE, STAFFORDSHIRE AND

48 FISHING IN THE MANIFOLD,
WETTON MILL, STAFFORDSHIRE

in the woods, to revert for a while to the primitive. The main point is that National Parks are natural playgrounds, where people have freedom to enjoy themselves in the open air. Therefore do not confuse them with wild-life sanctuaries and National Forest plantations (quite necessary institutions also), as these obviously cannot be playgrounds for the general public, and the restrictions necessary for their protection would impinge on that freedom which is the necessary basis of the National Park idea. And since in such a small country as ours even the waste spaces are in close relationship with agriculture, the National Parks will of necessity contain some farms and villages; the problem will be to balance public freedom of access with the rights of people striving to gain a livelihood there. (Though I should think they might find it more profitable to cater for visitors, and to work as wardens, foresters, etc.) The Parks could be made out of hills and moorlands unsuited for agriculture, unless it was rough grazing (sheep farming would not interfere); but in any case the preserving of certain areas for the enjoyment of the whole nation should be the first consideration. The rival claims of sport must also be considered when we are planning the countryside.

This country of the dales, south of the Wye, constitutes the district known as the Low Peak. Between it and the High Peak are marked differences, geological and historical. The High Peak is gritstone country of heathery moorland, the Low Peak is limestone pasturage; the High Peak was part of the Peverils' feudal domain, the Low Peak was always more democratic and its Barmoot Court upheld the rights of commoners against the aggressions of the great landlords. The Low Peak stretches as far south as Ashbourne; its area corresponds roughly with the Wapentake of Wirksworth, taking its name from the town which was the centre of the lead-mining industry. The lead mines were worked in Roman times and pigs of lead with Hadrian's mark on them have been discovered. There was a great demand for lead in the Middle Ages, for roofs, pipes and cisterns, and all this region is scarred with old lead workings. The mining district was known as the King's Field, and any man might search for lead there so long as he followed the laws and customs laid down by the miners' court. Some of these laws sound very curious to-day, but the men who made them had sound reasons for doing so. A man might dig anywhere save in house, church, road or garden, but to prevent him becoming a nuisance to private property he must find sufficient ore to fill a "dish," a standard measure holding fourteen pints; otherwise he was liable for damages. If he found sufficient ore the Barmaster, the official chosen by the miners to administer the industry, had to be informed. The finder was then awarded a "meer" or measure of land, which he must continue to work, or lose his privilege. The owner of the land had no power to remove him. A miner had to mark his claim by a "stow," a wooden frame used for hauling tubs of ore up the shaft. A thirteenth of all lead found went to the king (or his lessee), another portion went in tithes to the local clergy. The Barmaster and a jury of miners met twice a year in the Barmoot Court to settle disputes and regulate the industry. The small prospectors never formed themselves into a guild, and though some of them made fortunes, by 1600 most of them were reduced to the status of hired labour. The middlemen got control, the industry began to decline, and now only one mine of any importance is being worked. Water flooding the workings made production too costly to compete with foreign imports. A seventeenth-century poem gives an example of the old laws which the miners drew up:

> For stealing oar twice from the minery,
> The thief that's taken twice fined shall be,
> But the third time that he commits such theft,
> Shall have a knife stuck through his hand to th' haft,
> Into the stow, and there to death shall stand,
> Or loose himself by cutting loose his hand,
> And shall forswear the franchise of the mine,
> And always lose his freedom from that time.

Wirksworth, the capital of the Low Peak, is in a secluded valley a few miles from Matlock. It is a picturesque little town, and still keeps up the old custom of well-dressing at Whitsuntide, though here, instead of wells, they decorate the water taps with flowers. In the market place is the Hope and Anchor Inn, a very old hostelry with a new front, and inside a large Elizabethan mantelpiece carved with fleur-de-lys and the Tudor rose. A fifteenth-century priest's house, old houses and a grammar school line gardens facing old-fashioned brick cottages, with the church tower rising in the background. The nineteenth-century Moot Hall, where the Barmoot Court is held, is a small, single-storey structure with the miners' arms carved over the door: scales, pick and trough. Here is kept the massive brass dish used for measuring lead ore, made in the time of Henry VIII. The inscription on it states: "This Dishe to remayne in the Moote Hall at Wyrkysworth, hangying by a cheyne so as the Merchauntes or mynours may have resorte to the same at all tymes to make the true mesure after the same." It is said to be the only one of its kind in England. Wirksworth's cruciform thirteenth-century church was evidently meant to boast a large central tower, but somehow this never materialised; instead we have a squat tower crowned by a little spire many sizes too small. The church's greatest treasure is a Saxon coffin lid on which are carved forty figures illustrating scenes from the life of Our Lord. It is said to be eighth-century or earlier, and experts profess to find in it Roman and Byzantine influences. It measures five feet long by three wide, and was discovered in 1821 buried upside down near the altar; it is much decayed, but shows Christ washing the feet of the disciples, a cross with a lamb on it, a representation of the nativity, and other scenes.

The Low Peak is a region full of unexpected things. Among the confused hill ranges and winding rivers which have the trick of suddenly vanishing underground are little country towns and villages where old customs linger. At Ashford-in-the-Water (58) the curfew bell was rung, and the Pancake Bell on Shrove Tuesday. Hanging in the church are several paper garlands, for formerly it was the custom to hang them there when a girl died unmarried. Each garland is bell-shaped, with paper rosettes and streamers, and attached to each is a pair of gloves bearing the dead girl's name. Sometimes verses were written on them, but few are now decipherable. At the funeral all the unmarried girls of the village formed a procession and carried the garland to the church. Ashford is reputed to be the prettiest village in Derbyshire, and certainly its old bridges across the Wye form a lovely sight.

A mile or so down the Wye is Bakewell, an old Peakland town full of charm. It also possesses some fine old bridges, one a seventeenth-century packhorse bridge barely four feet wide, but has little to boast of in the way of ancient buildings. Known to the Romans and Saxons as a bathing-resort its reputation as a spa has long diminished, though the curious visitor can explore the old bath house built by the Duke of Rutland in the Bath Garden near the centre of the town. For the rest, Bakewell has some old gabled buildings and inns, some attractive almshouses known as Sir John Manners' Hospital, a seventeenth-century hall, and a market hall which would be quite picturesque had not its lower storey been disfigured by alterations. The church is a landmark for miles around, though the interior is disappointing (50). Its main attraction, of course, is the Vernon Chapel containing Dorothy Vernon's tomb; though the story of her elopement from Haddon Hall has not escaped the doubts cast on any romantic tale. The collector of curious epitaphs can ponder over such texts as "The day of a man's death is better than the day of his birth," or "By the grace of God I am what I am," over a half-wit's grave, nor must I omit mention of one extolling the virtues of a parish clerk who could say "Amen" better than anybody else. Near his grave is a Saxon cross, perhaps eighth-century, showing the usual scroll design and scenes from the life of Christ.

South of Bakewell winding roads lead over breezy moorlands to lovely Lathkill Dale and the forlorn village of Monyash. This was once the mining capital of the High Peak, as Wirksworth was of the Low Peak, but now it is little more than a collection of old stone houses and a seventeenth-century inn grouped round the village green. There are any number of these little clean-cut stone villages scattered about the uplands, and though they may not have the charm, say, of those in the Cotswolds, they are good to look at. Whether to call them villages or towns is a moot point, for the large village shades almost imperceptibly into the small town, so that it is hard to draw the line; perhaps Mr. Batsford's definition of *village town* might be applied to them. Winster is a good example, a typical Derbyshire hill settlement, with old houses that tell of its prosperity in lead-mining days. The church is mid-Victorian and ugly, but the tower is Georgian; the market hall, with filled-in arches, is perhaps 500 years old. Some villages, alas, have been spoiled by uncontrolled development, and others are long and straggling, but Tissington is almost perfect, and Parwich, Ashford, Alport and Edensor are worth seeing.

Following the Dove south through pleasant pastoral scenery you come to Hartington town or village—whichever you prefer; it had a market once—where an old hall and an older church face each other from opposite slopes. Hartington is a friendly, pleasant place though the local council's mania for asphalt and orderly kerbing has robbed it of a little of its charm. Gabled Hartington Hall was built in Shakespeare's time; now it is a youth hostel and young people in coloured shirts and shorts make merry where the Bateman family held sway for 300 years. The church is chiefly fourteenth-century, and apart from some unusual carvings on the west window is not very interesting, though personally I was intrigued by mention of the £4 a year which Mary Flint left for heating the stove in winter.

Hartington is a convenient centre for visiting Arbor Low, the stone circle on Middleton Common, which is often known as the "Stonehenge of the Midlands." Intending visitors should be warned not to expect anything spectacular. There are about forty stones, some up to twelve feet in length, lying inside a ditch and earthwork. All are flat on the ground, and whether they were part of a temple or burial place is open to question, though the evidence inclines to the latter. This region is rich in prehistoric remains, there being over a dozen tumuli within a two-mile radius and Saxon antiquities have been dug up from time to time. Three miles away is Youlgreave Church, which has an exquisite little alabaster tomb with a miniature effigy of Thomas Cockayne (died 1488); Chelmorton has a rare fourteenth-century stone chancel screen

A splendid avenue of limes leads into Tissington, famous for its ancient custom of dressing the wells on Ascension Day (39). It is a delightful little place of gardens and lawns and old houses, and a

[*From a drawing by J. C. Buckler, c. 1812*

50 BAKEWELL CHURCH, DERBYSHIRE,
    FROM THE SOUTH-WEST

51 SEVENTEENTH-CENTURY
MONUMENT TO SIR GEORGE
MANNERS, IN BAKEWELL
CHURCH, DERBYSHIRE

52 THE CHURCH AND GRAMMAR SCHOOL,
ASHBOURNE, DERBYSHIRE

53 THE ENTRANCE FRONT, SUDBURY HALL,
DERBYSHIRE, COMPLETED *c.* 1670

tiny church with a Norman tower rising above the yews and sycamores. The wells for which the village is celebrated come bubbling
out into stone troughs by the roadside. There are five and each has
its name, Hall Well, Town, Coffin, Hands and Yew Tree Wells.
They have not failed in the worst drought, and the purity of their
water is said to have saved the villagers from the ravages of the
Black Death. The well-dressing is supposed to be a thanksgiving
to commemorate that event, though some authorities declare it to be
a much earlier custom, perhaps a floral festival of pagan origin; to
sprinkle flowers upon a stream was an old way of propitiating the
water spirits. The "dressing" consists of a pictorial representation
of some Biblical scene ingeniously made of flowers, leaves, mosses
and rice on a framed clay background which is placed over the well
so that the water appears to issue out of the flowers. After the
service the vicar leads a procession round the wells and blesses
them. The custom, which was once a general one, is now confined
to Tissington, but was revived in other places when public wells
and taps were opened.

The road to Ashbourne passes through Fenny Bentley, whose old
manor house still retains the original square tower built by the
John Beresford who fought at Agincourt. He and his wife Agnes
have one of the most peculiar alabaster tombs in Derbyshire.
Evidently the sculptor was unable to portray their features accurately
so he depicted them both tied up in their shrouds, producing a most
bizarre effect. Charles Cotton said of Ashbourne that it had the
best malt and the worst ale in England. The old inn where Boswell
came with Dr. Johnson still survives—"a mighty civil gentle-
woman" was the landlady—though to its original name of the
Green Man has been added the additional one of the Black's Head.
Opposite the Elizabethan grammar school is the old brick mansion
where Dr. Johnson stayed with his friend John Taylor (52). Johnson's summer house still stands in the garden, but the grounds have
been altered since the days when the Duke of Devonshire came to
dine and Taylor ordered the coachman to drive twice round the
grounds to make the great man imagine they were larger than they
were, and Johnson tried to get rid of the dead cat—but let those
interested look up the details for themselves. Ashbourne Hall is
nothing much, though Bonnie Prince Charlie once slept there, and
was proclaimed king of England in the market place outside. The
parish church of St. Oswald has come in for a lot of exaggerated
praise. It is principally Early English, with additions, and local
patriotism refers to the octagonal spire 212 feet high as the "Pride
of the Peak." Among some interesting tombs and brasses lies the
recumbent figure of a child sculptured in white marble, the memorial
to Penelope Boothby which won lasting fame for Thomas Banks.

She lies there as though asleep, suggesting to Chantrey the idea of his "Sleeping Children" in Lichfield Cathedral. They still play the Shrove Tuesday football match in Ashbourne, though unsympathetic authority has banished it from the main thoroughfares. However, as the goals are about three miles apart and the game usually ends in Henmore Brook nobody minds very much.

We have wandered a long way from the High Peak, for the 1200-foot ridge of the Weaver Hills below Ashbourne marks the last southern outpost of the Pennines. Beyond are fertile farmlands stretching toward the Trent, fruitful Derbyshire Felix as it used to be called, to distinguish it from Derbyshire Deserta, the wild moorland region to the north. The Dove meanders south to join the Trent, but we must go back to the high hills for there is still one Peakland river to be explored—the Derwent. This is the dominant river of Derbyshire for it flows from north to south, cutting the county into almost equal halves. It rises on bleak Langsett Moor near the Yorkshire border and after taking tribute from a score of mountain streams has become quite a delightful river by the time it reaches Hathersage. Why no mention of Derwent or Ashopton villages lovers of the region may well ask, but, alas, these delightful spots are no more. In their place is the great new Ladybower Reservoir, which will convert the valley into a Derbyshire "Lake District." And a fine sight it now looks too, when full, with gleaming white concrete bridges towering above the blue water. The cottages of the new settlement are good to look at, but a little more imagination might have been shown in the layout of the place.

Hathersage was the "Morton" of Charlotte Brontë's *Jane Eyre*, which she named after an old Derbyshire family. Two houses claim to be the Moor House of the novel, though Moorseats has the better claim. Though much altered it is possible to identify places mentioned in the book. The church stands in lovely surroundings, and contains in the chancel the tomb of Robert Eyre who fought with Prince Harry at Agincourt. In the courtyard is the grave of Little John, Robin Hood's lieutenant, marked by two stones standing ten feet apart. Don't be a doubting Thomas! When the grave was opened in the eighteenth century it contained a thigh bone of unusual size. His house stood near by and his green cap and bow hung in the church, as the Oxford antiquarian Ashmole records in the time of James I. Each year members of the Ancient Order of Foresters, dressed in traditional Lincoln green, lay a wreath of laurel or cottongrass on his grave.

For forty miles the east bank of the Derwent is walled in by steep high moors, a succession of "edges" 1200 to 1400 feet high. "Edges" are the most typical feature of Derbyshire landscape, being

54 CHATSWORTH HOUSE, DERBYSHIRE, FROM THE AIR

55 BOLSOVER CASTLE, DERBYSHIRE, FROM THE WEST

["Country Life" photograph

56 THE STATE APARTMENT, CHATSWORTH HOUSE,
DERBYSHIRE, DESIGNED BY WILLIAM TALMAN, 1687

bold gritstone ridges which drop with startling abruptness into the valleys below. This wild border country, which the Hallam hunt used to scour on foot, contains many odd things of interest to the wayfarer, old monuments, stone circles, curiously shaped rocks, and some of the grandest views in England. Unfortunately local water boards exercise their democratic right by barring much of it to the general public, though they are not above renting portions to sportsmen for their private use. They justify this paradox by declaring that it helps the rates, forsooth! Sheffield Corporation is to be commended for keeping their part of the moors free and unspoiled.

On Hathersage Moor where Little John roamed is Carl Wark, a remarkable megalithic fortress walled in by ramparts of huge, unhewn stones. Home Guards had swept it with machine-gun fire and plastered it with bombs when I was last there. Incidentally the sign "Danger—Unexploded Shells" seems to be ousting the more familiar "Trespassers will be Prosecuted" as a method of keeping the ubiquitous proletariat from places where it isn't wanted. I hope this is not an omen of worse to come.

The sheep-dog trials held on near-by Longshaw Moor on the first Thursday in September are a recognised if informal social event, as the hundreds of cars parked about the old grey stone lodge used to testify. The trials take place in a semi-circle of rough moorland, marked by lines of hurdles, and here under the critical gaze of thousands of spectators, dogs whose training is a marvel of discipline show their skill. The shepherd stands there in apparent unconcern, and with an occasional whistle or signal directs the movements of his two dogs. It is their task to get half a dozen sheep into the pen unaided, and as the precious seconds tick away excitement grows tense. Now the sheep attempt to break through or double back, but quickly and surely the dogs coax them toward the goal. Success depends upon perfect co-operation and what sighs of relief and murmurs of applause arise as each lot is penned. Later the sheep-shearers show their skill, and specimens of their handiwork are exhibited. The thousand acres of Longshaw now belong to the National Trust, having been purchased by a group of Sheffield people for £22,000. Fox House Inn, where the sheep men retire for much-needed refreshment, stands at the cross-roads known as Whitecross, which readers of *Jane Eyre* will remember was the place where she alighted from the coach after her flight from Thornfield Hall.

It is a pleasant walk along the river to Padley Chapel, near Grindleford. Historically it is one of the most interesting places in Derbyshire. The chapel was formerly used as a cowshed, but has been restored by the Roman Catholic authorities, and each year a pilgrimage takes place there to honour Nicholas Garlick and Robert

Ludlan, two priests who were hanged, drawn and quartered in Derby in 1588. In a limestone gorge stands the picturesque village of Stony Middleton with its eighteenth-century octagonal church and houses rising tier upon tier among the rocky ledges. The hall was the home of the Denhams, one of whom used to breed black pigs and take them about in his carriage as presents for his friends. Another excused his lack of a coach by saying that the village in which he lived stood on end. On the outskirts is a Lover's Leap, better authenticated than most, where a lovesick girl jumped over the cliff, having carefully laid her hat on the grass first. As it happened she fell uninjured into a sawpit, and died many years afterward still unmarried.

So we come to Chatsworth, the seat of the present Duke of Devonshire (54). The world-famous "Palace of the Peak" stands in a deer park ten miles round, and is such an imposing place that it is usually described in superlatives. Originally it was a rectangular Palladian structure with a central court, to which was later added a long north wing which makes the building look somewhat lopsided; a south wing might remedy the defect. Viewed from across the woods and meadows the long front of the house bears an appearance of newness, though it dates from the seventeenth century, an impression due probably to the clean, creamy hue of the stonework and the imposing classical design. The house was begun by William Cavendish, afterwards first Duke of Devonshire, in 1687 and completed in 1707. The architect was William Talman, and the greatest artists of the day were called in to decorate it, Tijou to do the ironwork, Verrio the walls and ceilings. The wood carvings, formerly attributed to Grinling Gibbons, are now considered to be the work of Samuel Watson, a local man. Talman's handiwork has been often criticised and he had the not uncommon failing of building for show rather than comfort, but surely guests ought to be prepared to put up with a little discomfort in return for the privilege of staying at such a splendid residence? (56) Perhaps the north wing added in 1820–40 by Wyattville improved the amenity of the house even if it detracted from its appearance. Chatsworth is so full of treasures that it requires a book to itself, and to attempt to catalogue its wonders in a few hurried lines would be an injustice. Perhaps now the war is over it will again be open to the public, and you will be able to see the fifteenth-century tapestries, Thomas Hood's sham library, and the fiddle which people try to pick up only to discover that it is painted on the door. But before leaving Chatsworth I ought surely to mention that the original house on this site was one of Mary Queen of Scots' many prisons, and you can still visit her stone bower near the river.

After Chatsworth, Haddon Hall (page 5), which is not a great

57 ASHOVER BRIDGE ON THE RIVER AMBER,
DERBYSHIRE

58 THE BRIDGE OVER THE WYE,
ASHFORD-IN-THE-WATER, DERBYSHIRE

59   THE ENTRANCE FRONT, COMPLETED IN 1597

60 PORTION OF THE COLOURED FRIEZE IN THE STATE ROOM

HARDWICK HALL, DERBYSHIRE

distance away. Can you find anywhere such a contrast between two great houses? The one is an imposing classical mansion, the other a magnificently preserved example of medieval and Tudor domestic architecture. Haddon stands on a limestone escarpment above the wooded reaches of the Wye, one courtyard above the other, and its walls, turrets, towers and traceried windows incorporate all manner of styles from Norman to Jacobean. It is the result of centuries of building and rebuilding. Haddon has gripped the public's imagination by its association with the runaway match between Dorothy Vernon and John Manners.

Where the Wye runs into the Derwent stands Rowsley, chiefly famous for its old Peacock Inn, which was once a manor house. Near-by Darley Dale has a yew 2000 years old. The church is worth visiting for its Burne-Jones's *Song of Solomon* window, twelve panels which blaze with colour. From local quarries came the stone which paved Trafalgar Square and the Thames Embankment.

Matlock need not detain us long, for the approach along the main road shows industry in its most aggressive form. The place is the despair of all who like their natural beauty undefiled by turnstiles and tea-shops. Caverns, petrifying wells, pleasure gardens, automatic slot machines—all the usual "sights" are there for those who like that sort of thing. Matlock had some of the finest scenery in all England (High Tor which rises sheer 400 feet from the river is one of our grandest inland cliffs), scenery which moved Ruskin to raptures, and what has been done with it?—it has been commercialised into a bastard compound of quarries, limekilns, drab houses and hoardings. Matlock boasts of its beauty, but it appears to have sold its birthright for the proverbial mess of pottage. There is still some beauty left, thank Heaven, but it is best seen from the security of the neighbouring hills. There is a whole host of Matlocks but Matlock Bath is practically the creation of John Smedley, a hosiery manufacturer, who being convinced that doctors were either fools or knaves, declared the water cure to be the solution of all ills, and opened the celebrated Hydro in 1853. "Water is best" he was fond of declaring, and having made a fortune from the sale of water and air, was able to build Riber Castle for his home, on a hill above the town. Strangers still gape and inquire what institution it is.

Another man who built himself a castle in this neighbourhood was Sir Richard Arkwright, the inventor of the spinning-jenny, who founded cotton mills at Cromford in 1771. Cromford can therefore claim to be the origin of the modern factory system. The town is finely situated with its church, houses and fortress-like mills nestling beneath the precipitous Black Rocks (that Mecca of the week-end cragsman), but Willersley Castle lies across the Derwent.

NMC : H*

To Arkwright must go the credit for the wonderful woodlands which make this valley such a delight, for he planted 50,000 trees a year for seven years, for the enjoyment of posterity. A mile or so away at Holloway is Lea Hurst, a pleasant nineteenth-century house which was the home of Florence Nightingale.

The woods stretch for miles along the Derwent, and from the steep hills which line the river there are unforgettable views of the unbroken green canopy and the winding stream below. How I love those woods and hills! From every point the golden cap of Crich Stand shows up against the sky, and the dim blue hills of the Amber Valley stretch wave upon wave into the far distance. The River Amber (57) leads into a district which is not so attractive, for much of the country on the borders of Nottinghamshire is devoted to industrial purposes, and blast-furnaces and collieries have left their mark. The region contains a number of fairly large towns, Ripley, Ilkeston, Heanor, Clay Cross and Alfreton, but the untouched country in between has several places of interest. Between Ambergate and Alfreton is Wingfield Manor, once a prison of Mary Queen of Scots, now a remarkable ruin of a great fifteenth-century house. It was from this fortified mansion that Anthony Babington, who lived at Dethick near by, attempted to rescue the royal prisoner, a piece of foolhardiness which cost him his head. The house was begun by Ralph, Lord Cromwell, in 1441, and after being twice besieged during the Civil War was ordered to be dismantled by another Cromwell just over 200 years later. The order was not obeyed very faithfully, and had not a later owner pulled down part of the structure in order to secure the ready-dressed stone for a new building, the mansion would have been in an almost perfect state of preservation. But it is still one of the most fascinating ruins in England. Towering skyward atop a steep escarpment, like a fairy palace, stand the roofless banqueting hall and high watch tower, and great stone gates and guard-chambers rise forlornly above the grass-grown quadrangles.

Chesterfield is the second-largest town in Derbyshire, and owes its prosperity to George Stephenson, who lived here while supervising the construction of the Midland line; he is buried at Holy Trinity Church. Coal and iron, engineering, potteries and surgical dressings are among the town's varied products, but the visitor is more likely to be interested in the Tudor timbering and gables of the old buildings about the market place; much of it is sham, but those in the Shambles are 400 years old. The pride of the town is the fourteenth-century parish church, which has some colourful modern glass and old alabaster ornaments. Chesterfield is, of course, the town of the crooked spire. The story goes that the Devil seated himself on the steeple one night and the wind was blowing so hard that he had to twist his tail round it to avoid being blown away. Suddenly he heard a Chesterfield woman telling the truth, and this so surprised him that he flew off in a great hurry, without waiting to untwist his tail, and so the steeple got bent. Anyway, that is the yarn as it was told me. The steeple leans nearly eight feet out of the perpendicular, and for those who prefer a more prosaic explanation the distortion is said to be due to the warping of the timberwork under the lead covering. Inside the church the seeker after curiosities can find the bones of the identical dun cow killed by Guy of Warwick, though the sceptical are apt to affirm that it is the jawbone of a small whale. But what is the jawbone of a whale, large or small, doing in a church, anyway? The jawbone of an ass now—but that's a different matter!

The country between Chesterfield and the Yorkshire border is mainly industrial, but it has its picturesque moments. Norton was the birthplace of Chantrey, the great sculptor who began life as a Sheffield milk boy, and though Yorkshire has seized his native village he will always be regarded as a Derbyshire man. Whittington contains the "Revolution House" where in 1688 a group of men led by the Earl of Devonshire plotted to place William of Orange on the throne of England. But every little village in these rolling hills where the three counties meet seems to hold something of interest, and we cannot possibly explore them all. Sherwood Forest is our goal, and the best of it is contained in that area of great houses and woodlands known as the Dukeries. Derbyshire maintains till the last her high architectural standard, for where the steep hills merge into Nottinghamshire are three of the finest houses in England, Barlborough and Hardwick Halls and Bolsover Castle. These, together with the great houses of the Dukeries, Welbeck, Clumber and Thoresby, with neighbouring Rufford Abbey, enshrine some of the finest architecture we possess. Can any other area in England, I wonder, show such a splendid group of great houses?

Hardwick Hall, eight miles south of Chesterfield, is one of several mansions owned by the Duke of Devonshire (59). It is a grand old house in the Elizabethan style, having been finished in 1597 by that remarkable woman Elizabeth, Countess of Shrewsbury, otherwise known as "Bess of Hardwick." "Building Bess," as she has also beeen called, had a passion for building mansions, and being wealthy enough to gratify her tastes she built the first Chatsworth House, part of Bolsover, Oldcotes and many less-known buildings. A fortune-teller prophesied that she should not die until she stopped building, hence her incessant efforts to keep the workmen busy, but at last, ten years after the building of Hardwick a sharp frost brought all work to a standstill, and before it ended she died. Hardwick Hall—sole survivor of this energetic lady's building activities—

is a parallelogram in grey stone, with six towers each a hundred feet high, and windows occupying almost the whole of its long front. Local legend has it that there are as many windows as there are days in the year, thus giving rise to the couplet:

> Hardwick Hall,
> More glass than wall.

The house stands on a wooded height, and the sunlight flashing on its lofty towers and windows lights the place up like a beacon. The house is strongly impressed with the personality of its foundress, for where there is no glass the walls are decorated with the initials E.S. carved in stone a yard high, with a coronet over them; evidently the old dame did not mean to be forgotten in a hurry. Hardwick is principally noted for its old unique tapestries, furniture chiefly of the time of James II, and some 200 portraits of the Cavendishes and kings and queens of England, whose value is more historical than artistic.

A remarkable woman was Bess of Hardwick, perhaps after her friend Queen Elizabeth the most remarkable woman of her age. Biographers agree in describing her as "a proud, selfish and intriguing woman, a money-lender, a dealer in coals, lead and timber, who died immensely rich and yet without a friend." She began life as the daughter of a plain country squire, married four times, built innumerable mansions, died worth £60,000 a year, and was the founder of the three great ducal families of Devonshire. What a character for a novel! She was born in 1518, and John Hardwick, her father, was a man of such moderate means that she received only forty marks as her marriage portion. But Bess was ever a shrewd and ambitious dame, and at the age of fourteen she married Robert Barlow, a youthful neighbour, who died the following year leaving her his estate. This was the first of the four marriages which were to lead her to fame and fortune. At the age of thirty-one she married Sir William Cavendish, by whom she had six children, and having induced him to sell his estates in Suffolk, started her building career by building a mansion on the site of the present Chatsworth House. When her second husband died she married Sir William St. Loe, a Westcountryman, and having stipulated that all his estates should pass to herself and her heirs, when he died she acquired another fortune and his children by his first wife were left penniless. Then, at the age of fifty, she made her fourth matrimonial venture, marrying the sixth Earl of Shrewsbury, and thus becoming one of the richest and most powerful women in England. But scheming was in her blood, and though her own ambitions were achieved she could not rest content until her children were success-fully married too. In this she overreached herself when she arranged that her daughter Elizabeth should marry Charles Stuart, Earl of Lennox. For the only child of this marriage was Lady Arabella Stuart, who would be heiress to the thrones of England and Scotland if anything should happen to Queen Mary's son James. Faced with a possible rival Elizabeth vented her rage on the match-making mother and Bess went to the Tower, but she soon schemed her way out. She lived another thirty years or so, but there is no space to tell of her quarrels with her husband over Queen Mary, of their separation, of how she cut her children out of her will. She continued to scheme and build until the end, and is buried at All Saints' Church, Derby, under a monument which she designed herself.

Six miles north of Hardwick is Bolsover Castle (55), another Cavendish stronghold, part house, part ruin, crowning a steep crag 600 feet above the sea. It is a square, lofty pile like a Norman keep, with turrets at each corner, surrounded by old ramparts. It was built in 1613-17 by Bess of Hardwick's younger son, Sir Charles Cavendish, on the site of a Norman structure erected by William Peveril; the present house is an exact counterpart of the original. It dominates the wide Vale of Scarsdale, and the drowsy, decayed little market town at its foot. The inhabited part of the castle contains some thirty rooms, notable for their vaulted ceilings, ornamented fireplaces and walnut panelling and decorations; one is called the Star Chamber after that infamous apartment at Westminster, others are known as Heaven and Hell because of the varying themes portrayed on their painted ceilings. Beside the castle stand the roofless ruins of a palace erected by yet another of the "building Cavendishes" where Charles I and his queen witnessed the first performance of Ben Jonson's masque *Love's Welcome*; on that occasion William Cavendish spent £18,000 entertaining his royal guests. Ten years later Cromwell's cannon ended its career as a fortress.

Barlborough Hall, built by Francis Rodes in 1583, is a fine Elizabethan house whose battlemented walls and turrets are approached by a beautiful avenue of lime trees.

If you want to see the best of the old forests of England you must seek them in the private parks of the great landowners. Inside the aristocratic precincts known as the Dukeries, a stretch of country seven or eight miles square containing the three great estates of Welbeck, Clumber and Thoresby (owned respectively by the Dukes of Portland and Newcastle, and Earl Manvers), lie some of the most beautiful woodlands in all Britain. Besides the interest attaching to the great houses and families, these parks have the added interest that they contain all that is left of the ancient Forest of Sherwood (5). Once it measured twenty-five miles by ten, and stretched into

Derbyshire and Yorkshire; now the best of it is contained in Birk-
lands and Bilhalgh Forests, in Thoresby Park, where according to
tradition are oaks dating back to Robin Hood's time. From here
came the oaks for Cromwell's navy and timber for building St.
Paul's. A wonderful place it is in the early spring, when the oaks
and the birches have unfolded their first leaves, or the bluebells are
out. For those who like an historical flavour the wooded glades
and undulating parklands still retain something of the atmosphere
of Robin Hood and his Merry Men, and the diligent explorer can
discover many associations with this semi-legendary figure. At
Cresswell Crags is a cave which he used as a refuge, at Edwinstowe
he and Maid Marian were married, at Fountain's Dale was the cell
where Friar Tuck lived, and you can still see the well into which
Robin was tumbled after their hectic fight with quarter-staves.
Blidworth, in the heart of the forest area, is the burial place of
Will Scarlett. Trees of individual fame belonging to the old Sherwood Forest are the Major Oak, near Edwinstowe, a veteran with
a trunk thirty feet round; the 750-year-old Greendale Oak, which
was once so large that a carriage road was cut through its trunk,
is now propped up; Robin Hood's Larder near by was also known
as the Slaughter Tree because a sheep stealer used to hang stolen
carcasses inside. The famous Duke's Walking Stick is gone and the
Parliament Oak nearly so. Ollerton has some fine beeches (as well
as its old Hop Pole Inn).

Of the three mansions constituting the Dukeries, Welbeck Abbey
is mostly seventeenth-century, though built on the site of a monastic
establishment founded 500 years earlier. It is a large battlemented
house overlooking a lake, and Horace Walpole's description of its
interior is still worth quoting: "Oh, portraits! It is impossible to
describe the bales of Cavendishes, Harleys, Holleses, Veres, and
Ogles; every chamber is tapestried with them; nay, with ten thousand
other fat morsels, all their histories inscribed, all their arms, crests,
devices, sculptured on chimneys of various English marbles in
ancient forms (and, to say truth, most of them ugly). Then such a
Gothic hall, with pendant fretwork in imitation of the old, and with
a chimney piece extremely like mine in the library. Such water-
colour pictures! such historic fragments! But it is impossible to
tell you half of what there is." The fifth Duke of Portland had two
passions, building and privacy, and it was he who constructed the
underground ballroom and other subterranean apartments which
now constitute one of the "wonders" of this district.

Clumber House was built in 1772, and rebuilt in the classical style
after a disastrous fire in 1879. The interior is rich in art treasures,
china, manuscripts, books and pictures. But perhaps the finest
thing about it is the Duke's Drive, a wonderful avenue of lime trees

nearly three miles long. I cannot leave Clumber without mention of the third Duke of Newcastle, to whom belongs the rare distinction of never allowing anyone caught poaching on his estate to be prosecuted. When one remembers the savage game laws in force during the first half of the nineteenth century, when a sort of civil war was being raged between landowners and local countrymen, and even gleaning was called stealing, his attitude is even more remarkable. It is recorded that only once did he prosecute a poacher, and that was for killing hares in the close season.

The present Thoresby House was built in the Elizabethan style in 1864–70, to take the place of a Georgian predecessor destroyed by fire. Rufford Abbey, which is usually included in the Dukeries though not within the actual boundary, has suffered a fate common to many great estates, for it was sold for piecemeal development shortly before the war. Parts of the Forest area had already been spoiled by unplanned development, though some of the new settlements built by colliery companies were well designed. Two miles south-east is Eakring, to which William Mompesson came from the plague village of Eyam, and was forced by the villagers to live in a hut in the woods. He held weekly services under an ash tree, the site of which is now marked by a stone cross.

Worksop Manor is no longer a Dukery, though it formerly possessed this distinction until sold by the Duke of Newcastle. The original building was intended to be the biggest palace in England, and though only part of it was completed is said to have contained 500 rooms. In 1850 the then Duke of Newcastle decided it was not worth its upkeep, and pulled the whole place down; the present residence was constructed out of the stables. The manor is held by the tenure of providing a glove for the King's right hand at coronation and supporting it while he holds the sceptre, a tenure moved to this place from Farnham Royal, near Windsor. Worksop itself is an unpretentious little town which formerly had "a great produce of liquorice." On the outskirts are the remains of ancient Radford Priory, the Norman nave of which serves as the parish church. It is very similar in style and general appearance to Southwell Cathedral. The ruined lady chapel beside it is fine Early English work, but the finest thing of all is the gatehouse. It is a lovely old building, with a guest room and small chapel for the use of travellers, and has been a war memorial since 1929.

The district adjoining the forest on the south is a place of pilgrimage for Byron lovers, for Newstead Abbey and Annesley Hall are names to conjure with. Newstead stands beside a shining lake and there is a dream-like quality about its dark woodlands and bracken-covered hills suitably befitting its poetic qualities. It was a priory rather than an abbey, but for many years has been known less as the remains of a great Augustinian establishment than as the home of one of England's most famous poets. Pilgrims to Newstead probably know more about the place and the poet than I can adequately describe here, so they must read elsewhere of the "Merry Monks of Newstead" or the doings of the ghostly friar. Though the abbey and Byron relics belong to Nottingham Corporation the building was closed to the public for the duration of the war. Now they can again visit the grounds and gardens, see the oak which Byron planted in 1798, and the momument to Boatswain, his retriever, beside whom he wished to be buried. From the lakeside there is a fine view of the house and the wonderful Decorated west front of the fourteenth-century priory church adjoining the main entrance. It is certainly a beautiful scene, and well worth the modest sixpence charged. It is an intriguing district altogether if you study the map (how did the words *water* and *beck* for a stream come to be used in this part of England?) and old villages like Blidworth and Papplewick are worth a visit. Papplewick has carved coffin stones over 700 years old, while Blidworth has a curious "register of rockings," an old custom which has been recently revived. Once a year, on the first Sunday in February, the last baby boy to be christened is rocked in a cradle in the sanctuary.

At Hucknall Torkard Byron is buried, under a marble floor tablet presented by George I of Greece. Mansfield, which Leland described as "a praty market town," is now a thriving industrial centre, surrounded by coalfields, noted only for some curious cave dwellings carved out of the soft sandstone.

North of the forest the rolling farmlands stretch away to the Lincoln and Yorkshire borders; it is a district little visited by outsiders. East Nottinghamshire is predominantly agricultural, a district of meadowlands, orchards and cornfields, with busy market towns at intervals of ten or fifteen miles. The Great North Road sweeps across it in lordly fashion and old boroughs like Retford which once were places of call in coaching days now perform the same function for motorists. The other great highway is the Trent, a navigable tidal stream by which merchandise is conveyed to the Humber and the port of Hull. Some rather pretty scenery can be found in the triangle Bawtry—Blyth—Clayworth, but the area contains few show places; its atmosphere is that of the districts further east and already one senses the proximity of the lowlands and the fens. From Gringley-on-the-Hill one can look across endless miles of flats, or carrs, as they are called, which were once a dreary swamp land regularly flooded at every spring tide. Everton is a village of red roofs and winding lanes, and Blyth is old and lovely, with one of the oldest churches in the county and one of the oldest inns in England. (It had a recorded history of three

62   THE STANLEY PALACE, CHESTER

61   THE FISHING PAVILION IN BERESFORD DALE,
DERBYSHIRE. BUILT IN 1574 BY CHARLES COTTON,
AND USED BY HIMSELF AND IZAAK WALTON

63 CHESTER CATHEDRAL

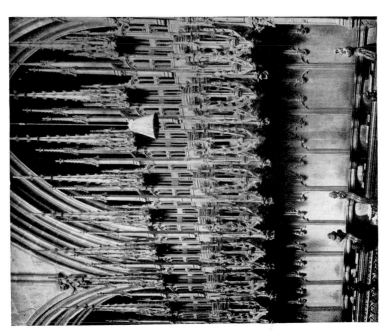

64 NANTWICH CHURCH

LATE GOTHIC CRAFTSMANSHIP IN CHESHIRE QUIRE STALLS

centuries when Leland stayed there in Henry VIII's time.) Celia
Fiennes, who rode through England on a side-saddle in the reign
of William and Mary, wrote of Blyth Hall that it "was a very sweet
house and garden and grounds, and the fine river by it with fish
ponds and meadows and fine woods beyond makes it look very
pleasant; it's very ffruitefull—I eate good fruite there." Near Blyth,
at a hamlet with the entrancing name of Styrrup, is the site of a
medieval tournament ground, one of the five licensed tilting places
in England. Scrooby, which is a rather dull little place clustered
about its church, is better known to Americans than to English
people, for it was the home of William Brewster, one of the two
leaders of the Pilgrim Fathers. A so-called vicarage, a room in the
manor house which Brewster used, the "Brewster" pew in the
church—these are scanty enough evidence around which to weave
a sentimental association, but the eye of faith sees further than
mere logic. Of the archiepiscopal palace where Wolsey came after
his fall from grace there is even less to see, though a mulberry tree
said to be of his planting is still pointed out; here again a little faith
is necessary. There is more to see at ruined Mattersey Priory, a
small house founded by the Gilbertines about 1185.

But of all the old-world villages strewn casually over the green
Nottinghamshire countryside none is more interesting historically
than Littleborough, that nocturne in red beside the silvery Trent.
As a place it is nothing much, a few farms, a few cottages, a tiny
stone church, but it has that quality of agelessness that makes some
of our English villages a joy to see. Here King Harold and his men
crossed the river on their way to Hastings, by the ferry which is
said to have been used without a break since Roman times; the
oldest ferry in England, they'll tell you. And if you watch by the
bank during the spring tides you'll see the Aegir, or bore, a wall of
water six feet high come rushing up the river and causing consterna-
tion among the boatmen. But if you remember your *Mill on the
Floss* you'll know all about this, for the Floss is the Trent, and the
town of St. Ogg's is Gainsborough across the river. But there we
shall not go.

North of Littleborough the river meanders on through the flat
lands, there are a few more villages, then the Trent flows out of the
Midland region and into other scenes.

FROM MERSEY TO THE TRENT

Cheshire is known as the county of the dairy farmer and its
grassy landscapes with their grazing cattle constitute the traveller's
typical impression of the region. It is also a county of several large
towns and industries, but this fact is not so widely realized. Some

of the towns have populations of over 100,000, and Cheshire salt and silk are almost as widely known as are its dairy products. Crewe is a household word, synonymous with railway; in fact I am not certain that I oughtn't to begin this account of the North Midland countryside at Crewe, for every railway traveller must have visited the place at least once. But Crewe is one of those places which millions of people pass through and never see (what are your impressions?), and though there may be a fascinating hidden life there, I prefer to start with Chester. Though it is not the largest town, it is the county town, for good historical reasons. Rare old Chester they call it, and of course the visitor is expected to enthuse over its walls, castle, cathedral, rows and old houses. Actually it isn't difficult to enthuse, for Chester is unique; it is the only completely walled town we have left in England.

But I chose it for reasons other than these. It isn't very centrally situated for a county town, but its situation was responsible for its prominence in history until the coming of the industrial era. The city stands on a rocky sandstone spur where the Dee makes a wide curve; it has been successively fortress, port, frontier outpost, and cathedral and market town. Roman, Briton, Saxon, Dane and Norman have all dwelt here and all have left their mark. The place is sheer epitomised history. Of course its greatest attraction is its walls, which almost completely encircle the older part of the town. (Needless to say a great portion of the modern city lies outside.) The walls are of red sandstone and are nearly two miles round. They are built upon Roman foundations, though the upper portions have been many times renewed. They vary from twelve to forty feet in height and form a raised promenade from which the town may be viewed. Every so often they are pierced by gates or strengthened by towers. From the walls it will be seen that the town retains the original rectangular form of the camp built by Ostorius Scapula in A.D. 47 (called Deva after the river; the Britons called it Caerleon); with a gate in the centre of each of the four sides and streets leading directly from the gates to the military headquarters in the centre. Chester was a Roman city for more than 300 years, and in the Grosvenor Museum you can study inscribed stones and other interesting objects telling of the exploits of the celebrated 20th Legion, known as Valeria Victrix. When the Romans left, the town was destroyed by the Northumbrians and lay in ruins for another 300 years. The Saxons rebuilt it, and it was the last town in England to hold out against the Normans (just as, nearly six centuries later, it held out against Cromwell). But space is too short to tell all of Chester's exciting history; you must look it up for yourself. Each building and alleyway seems to have its story.

Various theories have been propounded about the origin of the

Rows, that remarkable feature of Chester architecture. They are believed to have been derived from the arcades of the north Italian towns, or even from the original Roman buildings. The special characteristic of the Chester Rows is not, however, the covered pavement, but the rows of shops on the second storey. There is nothing like them anywhere else in England; the only example of a similar arrangement is the main street of Thun, in Switzerland, which has a double series of shops on either side, one above the other. One theory is that originally the streets of Chester were lined with ruined Roman buildings, that traders built their shops on top of this heaped-up debris, that gradually the second storeys of the buildings were thrust forward on wooden posts so that the pavement became roofed over. Access was by stairs or steps at regular intervals. Other traders built booths underneath which in time became permanent shops, so that eventually there materialised the Rows with their two storeys of shops.

In addition to the general old-fashioned appearance of the Rows there are some fine old half-timbered houses (62) with carved and decorated fronts, including some in that style of ornamental plaster-work known as "pargetting." Among the best are Bishop Lloyd's Palace, God's Providence House (so named because it was the only building which escaped the plague when the city was depopulated), and the Stanley Palace. Leche House, perhaps the least-known, must be included among the six best specimens of sixteenth- and seven-teenth-century timberwork. Its plasterwork, incorporating the royal arms, is probably the finest in the city. Chester has also several celebrated inns, of which the old seventeenth-century Falcon Inn (now a café) is a lovely black and white building, well restored.

Chester Cathedral is a splendid example of a monastic church, for it was an abbey from late in the eleventh century until the dissolution of the monasteries. The view from the walls shows its three main features—the massive central tower, the huge south transept, and the steep pyramid roof of the lady chapel. The richly decorated stonework has an appearance of newness hardly in keeping with its venerable age, having been refaced last century. There is no trace of the original Saxon church, but the base of the north-west tower is Norman, as is also the small north transept, and the north aisle of the nave. The nave is one of the smallest of any English cathedral, the south transept one of the largest. The lady chapel and chapter house, both Early English, were added in the thirteenth century; the choir dates from about 1300. The Jacobean period is represented by the south-west tower, which serves as the Consistory Court. The cloisters where the monks studied and meditated are good Perpendicular work, and their unusual position on the north instead of the south side of the nave was probably owing to a grant of land having been made in that direction. Adjoining them is a vaulted Norman chamber believed to have been the abbot's entertaining hall. The thirteenth-century refectory contains one of the finest examples of a lector's pulpit that exists, the only one like it being at Beaulieu in Hampshire. The cathedral is not rich in monuments, but among its possessions which are worth seeing are the sixth-century font from north Italy, the choir stalls (63) whose splendid canopies and carved miserere seats dating from about 1385 rank with those of Lincoln, the modern high altar of carved oak, cedar and olive, the modern mosaics in the nave, and the restored St. Werburgh's shrine with figures showing the royal house of Mercia.

Chester has several other notable churches. St. Peter's is built on the masonry of the Roman *Praetorium*. The fine Norman church of St. John the Baptist is the legendary refuge of King Harold after his defeat at Hastings. The medieval chapel of St. Nicholas has become a cinema, and St. Olave's Church, with its memories of the Danish conquest, is disused.

But now it is time to leave Chester, without even mention of its castle, crypts, or other wonders. I am acutely conscious of the shortcomings of this very inadequate description, but blame the war and the paper shortage! The town needs a book to itself.

A favourite excursion from Chester is by river steamer to Eaton Hall, the nineteenth-century Gothic palace of the Duke of Westminster. Everything here is on an immense scale, from the clock tower which is an imitation Big Ben to the library nearly a hundred feet long. The intricate eighteenth-century ironwork of the Golden Gates is by the brothers Roberts.

To the north-west of Chester, between the estuaries of the Dee and the Mersey, is the Wirral Peninsula. It is a pleasant, undulating country of meadows and woodlands with winding roads leading to quaint villages, each with some claim to our notice. Parkgate was the home of Grenfell of Labrador, and also of John Speed the tailor, who was England's first historian. Burton was the home of Thomas Wilson, who claimed with justification that he was the poorest bishop in Europe; Neston knew Nelson's Lady Hamilton. But if Runic stones (Upton), old crosses and petrifying springs (Bromborough) or the footprints of prehistoric Labyrinthodons (Storeton and Bebington) are not to your taste then try the sandhills and wild saltings which stretch for miles along the coast. There you can be as lonely as anywhere in England. I remember as a boy idling away the sunny hours on the red rocks of the Hilbre Islands, between England and Wales, waiting for the tide to go out and reveal whether the lines I had set had caught any dabs for dinner. There was a fascination about that coast with its sweeping distances

65   BEESTON CASTLE, CHESHIRE

66   THE DANE VALLEY, NEAR WINCLE, CHESHIRE

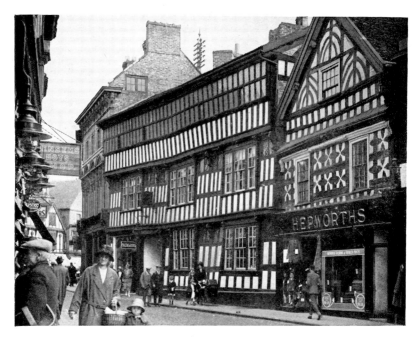

67 THE CROWN INN, NANTWICH, CHESHIRE

68 BRAMHALL OLD HALL, CHESHIRE

and swirling tides and sands, though to the more sophisticated its scenery might be nothing much. The Sands o' Dee are aptly named, and I have known what it is to scramble hastily ashore through the swiftly rising tide. If you like a quieter version of the English seaside resort Hoylake and West Kirby may take your fancy.

Wallasey, of course, is Liverpool's extra bedroom where she lodges those people for whom there is not sufficient air in her murky streets. When we lads clattered in our clogs down the Guinea Gap to watch the *Lusitania* go out on her last voyage it was a string of independent townlets, Seacombe, Egremont, New Brighton and others, but now it has blossomed into a great dormitory town of over 100,000 people. Above Wallasey the Mersey banks are devoted to industry; industry at its most aggressive, as at Birkenhead; industry with its social conscience developed, as at Port Sunlight. There the estuary broadens out into a wide inland sea whose mud flats and low-lying marshlands have that air of forlorn loneliness common to places possessed of far-reaching horizons. A remote desolate place where you can tramp for miles undisturbed, the only sounds the crying of the gulls as they soar over the canal where the great ships come to Manchester. How odd a sight to see 15,000-tonners steaming sedately through the green Cheshire countryside. Exactly how remote it all is is expressed in the phrase "Go to Ince!" for to reach that marsh-surrounded village was often tantamount to accomplishing the impossible. Ince, of course, is really Ynys or Innis, the Island. Best of the little ports is Runcorn, with its heronry and hills of flowering broom. It is one of those intimate little ports where you can feel at home with the seamen who lean over the rails of the steamers in the canal telling highly coloured tales. But the great attraction of Runcorn was that it was the last home of the square-rigged sailing ship in England. Before the war you could sometimes see as many as half a dozen little windjammers moored in the harbour. They used to bring cargoes of china clay from the West Country, returning with coal. The last square-rigger I saw entering Runcorn was the barquentine *Waterwitch* of Fowey. When Trinity House required all London pilots to have training in a square-rigged sailing vessel scores of young men served aboard her in order to secure their pilot's "ticket." Where is the *Waterwitch* now, I wonder?

If I were asked what part of Cheshire most expressed the spirit of the county I should choose the range of sandstone heights stretching across the centre from Frodsham by the Mersey to Malpas near the Flintshire border. This is the most delightful country imaginable, not the typical Cheshire of imagination, of course, for here are hills standing boldly against the skyline, their steep slopes heavily forested or showing bare red rock. It is un-English land-

scape, more like something from the Continent, say the Black
Forest; personally I always think of it as the "Land of Castles"
for each summit seems to have its grey-walled fortress. Look
upward from the Tarporley road and see Beeston Castle on its
rock (65) and beyond it the grey keep of Peckforton Castle rising
above the treetops and you will understand what I mean. But the
touring public seems to pass it by. Beeston Castle is one of the
finest sights I know, as good as anything the Rock of Cashel can
show. There on top of a sheer wall of rock 400 feet above the plain,
defended by moat, gates, walls and massive round towers, is the
stronghold built by the Earl of Chester in 1220. Seekers after buried
treasure might care to try their luck in the castle well, cut through
solid rock for 366 feet; legend says it's there.

The range is known by various names throughout its length.
From Halton with its old castle standing like a Rhineland fortress
above the "Narrows" of the Mersey, the hills sweep southward.
There are fragmentary remains of castles at Rock Savage and on
Overton Hill above Frodsham. The latter is a picturesque old town
built into the solid rock, with the Bear's Paw Inn dating back to
Stuart days. The town was the home of Francis Gastrell, who
destroyed Shakespeare's house to spite the Stratford Corporation.
South of Helsby Crag, with its curious likeness to a man's face, the
bald summit of Eddisbury Hill rises above the green glades of
Delamere Forest. Delamere was one of the three Norman forests
of Cheshire, though its area has diminished by two-thirds since the
enclosures of the last century. It still covers 4000 acres, and its
shady nooks and reedy lakes invite the wanderer in search of
solitude. Delamere is a naturalist's treasure house, and with what
delight have I watched the black-headed gulls on Oakmere bird
sanctuary, or hunted for wild rosemary and sundew plants. And I've
also spent several weeks with a party of archaeologists digging
among the ruins on top of Eddisbury Hill for some trace of the
town built there by Ethelflaeda, the warlike daughter of King
Alfred. We dug through a series of cultures but found no trace of
the Saxon *burh*.

The district south of Delamere has a number of old towns and
villages of the characteristic black and white architecture. It is also
a district of old halls and houses, too numerous to mention them all,
many built on the ruins of monastic establishments. Vale Royal,
home of Lord Delamere, contains fragments of one of the greatest
abbeys in England. Combermere Abbey stands on the site of a
twelfth-century Cisterican monastery, while Saighton Grange, like
a castle on its rock, was also part of a medieval abbey. The histories
of all these old mansions are inseparably associated with the names
of the families who built and lived in them. Cheshire was famed for

the number of its old families, and did not Speed say of the county that it was the "seedplot of gentility"? Or, as an old couplet puts it less delicately:

> As many Leighs as fleas, Massies as asses,
> Crewes as crows, and Devonports as dogs' tails.

But again it is time to cry halt, for it is hard to tear oneself away from this region of bracken-covered hills and dark woodlands and old houses. And I have not said a word about Tarporley, that little town of one long street with grim Ukinton Hall near by, or Malpas

[*Drawn by Brian Cook*

HOLFORD HALL, CHESHIRE

on the hill with its overhanging houses, and its church chest with decorated ironwork wrought by an unknown craftsman seven centuries ago. Nor have I spoken of the old customs which lingered in these out-of-the-way villages; rush-bearing at Farndon, heaving at Toft, and Barning (Adorning) the Thorn at Appleton.

Now Nantwich is a fine town, and the quaint, old-fashioned air of its narrow streets and timbered Elizabethan houses (67) sets one thinking of romance rather than of industry. Yet it was industry which produced the quaintness of Welsh Row and lovely Sweet Briar Hall, for formerly the town produced more salt than all the Cheshire springs put together. In Camden's time salt was the principal support of the town. "Nantwich, the first that is visited by the Weever, is called by the Welsh Hellath Wen, White-Salt-Wich, because the whitest salt is made here." The town has several times been destroyed by fire, which probably gave the Royalists the idea of firing red-hot shot among the houses during the Civil War. Among the black and white houses rises the red sandstone tower of the church, of the rare octagonal shape. Mainly Decorated and Perpendicular, its chief possessions are a medieval stone pulpit with stone screen to the chancel, and twenty carved oak stalls in the choir (64), said to have been brought from Vale Royal Abbey. These 500-year-old carvings and the alabaster knight on the altar tomb may attract the casual visitors, but to me the most poignant memorial was that to John Hornby, the young explorer who with two companions died of starvation by the Thelon River in the Canadian Arctic in 1927. It was the reading of their diary, years ago, which filled me with the desire to visit the Arctic and see the mighty Thelon River. This is a long way from Nantwich, whose other claim to notice is that it was the home of John Gerard, the herbalist.

North of Nantwich lies the Salt Country along the River Weaver, already described, and Crewe, where tourists pass but rarely stop. From Crewe it is a pleasant walk to Bartomley, where during the Civil War a party of Royalists drove twenty villagers into the church, set fire to it, and cut them down with their swords when they fled outside. It happened to be Christmas. Sandbach is not far away, another old town, known to antiquarians for its Saxon crosses. Old crosses may leave you cold, but these two are really unique. They are perhaps the finest things of their kind in England, and if they were situated in Ireland or Scotland people would go out of their way to visit them. To begin with their size is quite impressive, sixteen feet or so for the tallest, and the fact that they have survived 1300 years of war and weather ought to grip the imagination of the dullest. Of course they haven't stood in Sandbach's cobbled market place all that time undisturbed, for the Puritans knocked them down in the seventeenth century and used bits of them for walling or steps or paving-stones. Thanks to the enterprise of George Ormerod, the Cheshire historian, the pieces were all collected and put together again. The Saxon carvings are getting a bit weather-worn, but you can make out the Crucifixion scene, the manger at Bethlehem, Christ bearing the cross, while the smaller cross depicts scenes showing Peada, King of Mercia, on a missionary journey through the Midlands. It is believed the crosses were erected to commemorate his conversion to Christianity and his marriage to a Christian princess.

Situated among wooded parklands in mid-Cheshire is Knutsford, a busy place of narrow streets and some sixteenth-century cottages; it is the Cranford of Mrs. Gaskell. Westward lies the "country of

70 THE PERPENDICULAR INTERIOR,
ASTBURY, CHESHIRE

69 STUART CHANCEL STALLS,
CHOLMONDELEY, CHESHIRE

71   TISSINGTON HALL, DERBYSHIRE

[*From a drawing by C. J. Richardson*

72   GAWSWORTH HALL, CHESHIRE

the rhyming signposts," for Rowland Warburton, the master of Arley Hall, was known as the "rhyming squire." Some of the signposts he erected still bear his whimsical directions.

> This road is forbidden to all,
> Unless they wend their way to call,
> At Mill, or Green, or Arley Hall.

Another states:

> No cartway save on sufferance here.
> For horse and foot the road is clear,
> To Lymm, High Legh, Hoo Green or Mere.

Daresbury, home of Lewis Carroll, is only a few miles away. Northward is Altrincham, an old market town which has been the subject of some rude rhymes. De Quincey wrote of the market place that it was "the gayest scene I ever beheld," but that was before they made a level-crossing across the main street to vex motorists. Altrincham formerly had a mayor but no corporation, but as he was assisted by constables, market-lookers, chimney-lookers, dog-muzzlers, ale-tasters, and a bellman, one wonders what he did with his time. The bellman no longer goes round crying the daily news, his place having been taken by the ubiquitous B.B.C.

This district, watered by the Dane and Bollin rivers, is the typical Cheshire of lush pastures and hedgerows. It has everything that the British exile in foreign lands visualises when he thinks of England: green meadows and occasional ploughlands, spinneys and fox coverts, and enough lakes—meres, they call them—to make a miniature lake district. Some of the meres are quite large; Tatton Mere is three-quarters of a mile long and lies in a 2000-acre park. Rostherne's 100 acres, bordered by hanging woods, is perhaps the most delightful of all. Tabley Mere has an island with an uninhabited manor house 600 years old; the last Lord de Tabley was a keen naturalist and poet, and made the place into a sanctuary for plants and wild life. Bagmere by Brereton Hall was believed to tell the future, for when the master of the house was going to die trees would rise from the bottom of the lake and float on the surface. The hall is a fine brick building built in 1586, and there is a story that Queen Elizabeth laid the foundation stone.

But the chief joy of this part of Cheshire is its black-and-white "magpie" architecture, for here are some of the finest half-timbered houses in all England. Handforth Hall, built in 1562 by Uryan Brereton, is not all timber and plaster, but partly brickwork painted to represent the old style. Adlington Hall has black-and-white timbered gables and porch surrounding the Elizabethan courtyard, but the newer portion of brick and stone was added in 1757. It has a great hall with an open timbered roof, some fine carvings, and is partly surrounded by a moat. Chorley Hall, near Alderley Edge, is another half stone, half timbered structure, sixteenth-century, with a double-arched moat bridge. Scattered about the neighbouring countryside are several fine black-and-white farmhouses, formerly halls. Swineseye Farm's timbering suggests a date earlier than 1647, and Oldhall Farm near Woodford is another good example.

I have left till last the two finest specimens, for it is a very debatable point whether Bramhall Hall or Moreton Old Hall is the finest surviving timber house in Cheshire, perhaps in England. Certainly Bramhall (68) is a delight, for careful renovation and preservation have left the old house with all its ancient beauties. Originally it was owned by the Bromeales or Bromhals, but passed by marriage to the Davenports in Edward III's time. It shows traces of several periods, for though originally quadrangular in form the west wing was removed in 1819; of the remainder the north wing is thirteenth-century and the south fourteenth-century. Bramhall was the home of the Davenports for 500 years. They altered it in the sixteenth century, so that the great hall which was once open to roof now has an Elizabethan drawing-room over it. There is also a dining-room, private chapel, the Paradise room (so named from seventeenth-century tapestry representing the Fall of Man), and all the usual offices of an old-time house. But perhaps after all Moreton Old Hall (page 69), or Little Moreton Hall as it is variously known, is the finest of them all, even though it does appear a bit aslant. Seen from across the moat it is an intriguing collection of gables and leaded windows and dark overhangs; the traditional Gothic transferred from stone to wood. It is entirely surrounded by the moat, and access is gained by way of a stone bridge and a timbered gate-house that is itself one of the finest of its kind (3). The hall is a veritable palace in black and white, forming three sides of a quadrangle. The oldest portion is the chapel, and the great hall and long gallery contain big decorated fireplaces and ornamented woodwork; a variation of the Queen Elizabeth myth is that she not only slept but danced here. Perhaps the crowning glory of the hall is the wonderful bay windows overlooking the courtyard, dating from 1559, and the inscription "Richard Dale, Carpeder, made this window by the Grac' of God" records the builder's pride in his achievement.

Of black-and-white villages Prestbury, a mile or so from Maccles-field, is a delightful old-world place. It is just one street of houses, no two alike, an old inn, and a fourteenth-century Priest's House which is now the District Bank. (Is it coincidence that several banks appear to have undertaken the maintenance of various old black-and-white buildings? I have noticed several examples.) During the days of the Commonwealth a parson ejected from the local church used to preach from the gallery above the door. The school adjoining the church, originally the chapter house, has a grand Norman gateway dating from the late twelfth century. I could linger long in Prestbury, extolling its quaintness, but must spare a few words for Gawsworth, another enchanting village. Gawsworth has "the loveliest rectory in Cheshire," a black-and-white

[Drawn by Thomas Garratt

LITTLE MORETON HALL, CHESHIRE: A BIRD'S-EYE VIEW
OF GATEHOUSE AND COURTYARD

house of 1470; the medieval-looking hall with its tilting-ground is an alluring sight (72). Grappenhall is another old village, with stocks, thatched post office, and in the church an effigy in chain armour of Sir Fitzwilliam le Boydel, dating from 1275.

I cannot leave the subject of "magpie" architecture without mention of two unique black-and-white churches. Marton Church is built of massive wooden pillars and huge beams, and with its

NMC : K

shingled stumpy spire looks like something from Norway or Switzerland. Much of the timberwork is original fourteenth-century. Lower Peover's church has a sixteenth-century stone tower, but the nave and chancel are fourteenth-century timber and plasterwork; some of the great oak beams are said to date back to 1296. Among examples of woodworking skill are the pews with raised doors to keep out draughts, a Jacobean pulpit, and an ancient church chest cut from a solid oak log. Local girls were reckoned not fit to be a farmer's wife unless they could lift the lid with one hand. Many men can't lift it with two! Siddington church appears to be timbered but is really painted brick; the chancel is black and white.

The church at Wilmslow on the River Bollin also contains a chest carved from a block of oak four feet long, but its chief pride is a fifteenth-century brass depicting Robert le Bothe of Dunham and his wife. Wilmslow has changed greatly since Samuel Finney, the miniature painter, wrote of it in 1770 that the "people were eaves dropers" and "Fearings and boggarts lurk in every dark hole." Nowadays the greatest fear and danger—to a cyclist—are Bren-gun carriers and casual army lorries. Do Wilmslow folk still believe in boggarts?

Alderley Edge, a couple of miles south of Wilmslow, is a tree-clad sandstone ridge rising 650 feet above sea level. It is an intriguing place of old buildings and mine workings, just far enough from Manchester for lads to play truant from Sunday School on borrowed bicycles, as I know to my sorrow. For it was on a Sunday that I went alone down the tunnel of the great copper mine, and having lost my way in the dark had to sit with my legs dangling over a ledge until rescued. A few weeks later three young men got trapped on a further ledge and died there. Somewhere about here are iron gates leading to a huge cavern, where, according to tradition, a band of knights sleep with their horses tethered beside them. Is this a variant of the Arthurian myth?

A few miles east of Alderley the high moorlands rear themselves up like a wall. Cheshire is not quite so flat as many people imagine, for it pokes a narrow arm of territory clean into the heart of the Peak District. I first discovered this fact when I accompanied a rambler friend on "a bit of a walk round Cheshire." After we had climbed for what seemed hours and hours up a confoundedly steep hill, I burst out breathlessly: "But I thought Cheshire was *flat*?" "Then you thought wrong, m'son," grinned my companion. "Come along, we've only climbed seventeen hundred feet." That was on Shining Tor, 1833 feet. But the highest hill in Cheshire, curiously named Soldier's Lump, adjoining Black Hill overlooking Yorkshire, is nearly 2000. This wildest part of Cheshire is remote as anywhere

73 CHOLMONDELEY CHAPEL, CHESHIRE, FROM
THE SOUTH-WEST. RESTORED 1652

74 TOMB OF PHILIP MAINWARING, 1656.
HIGHER PEOVER, CHESHIRE

[From a drawing by J. C. Buckler, 1820]

75 TABLEY HOUSE, CHESHIRE

76 THE JACOBEAN DRAWING-ROOM,
LYME PARK, CHESHIRE

(THE PROPERTY OF THE NATIONAL TRUST)

in England. The River Etherow rushes down through desolate Longdendale Valley to join the Goyt coming from the high moors above Buxton; together they form the Mersey. The towns on the edge of the moors are really the overflow from the Manchester cotton industry; Hyde, Stockport and Stalybridge are respectably sized industrial towns and as such are fine places to escape to the "freedom" of the countryside. Twopennyworth on the local bus takes you to Lyme Park or Marple Hall; the wild country is never very far away. Lyme Hall (76) is one of the most beautiful Elizabethan and Classic houses in the county, and deserves more than passing mention. Out on the windswept moorlands, high above the world, you can forget that man or his works exist, for there will be only occasional grey stone farmhouses and curving drystone walls to remind you of his presence. If you would find peace, climb on a summer's day up the great hill leading to the Cat and Fiddle Inn, and then by way of Wildboarclough into the Dane Valley (66) to Wincle, a remote village that still gets cut off by snowdrifts during severe winters. It is erroneously believed that the Cat and Fiddle is the highest inn in England, but that honour is reserved for one on Tan Hill in Yorkshire. Still, 1690 feet is a respectable altitude at which to quench your thirst, isn't it?

All roads round here seem to lead to Macclesfield, a hilly, all up-and-down town, whose cobbles resound daily to the clatter of mill workers' clogs. But then everybody in this district wears clogs (I am wearing a pair as I type this; and very warm and comfortable they are, too). Macclesfield was once a walled and gated town, but now most of its old-time character has vanished; gaunt brick mills cluster about the steep hill crowned by St. Michael's Church. The town's main industry in the Middle Ages was button-making. Modern Macclesfield is the creation of Charles Roe, who started the first silk mill in 1756. The Franco-German war of 1870 brought prosperity to the town, for the French silk trade was in no position to compete. Fortunes were made, and Macclesfield took on an air of opulence which it retained long after the fortunes had been dissipated. But it is still the centre of the British silk trade.

St. Michael's Church is reached by 108 steps—or is it 140?—and though founded in 1278 by Edward I and his Queen Eleanor, was modernised in very patchy fashion in the eighteenth century. It is the only church I know where you can find a sedan chair (somebody who came to service a couple of hundred years ago must have absent-mindedly left it behind), or carved alabaster figures which have been blackleaded—yes, blackleaded! In the Savage Chapel is the Pardon Brass recording that Roger Legh and his six sons were to receive 26000 years and 25 days pardon in return for saying five paternosters and five aves. The tombs of the Savage family are imposing piles of alabaster and marble, with effigies of men who fought at Bosworth, Boulogne and many other places in the fifteenth and sixteenth centuries.

Congleton, a few miles away, is another silk town, though at one time its chief industry was glove-making. It has also lost most of its old buildings, though a few half-timbered houses survive. The old Cheshire adage "Congleton rare, Congleton rare, sold the Church Bible to buy a new bear" refers to a happening in the seventeenth century. The corporation had saved enough money to buy a new Bible for the church when the town bear died, and it was decided that the townsfolk would rather have a new bear than a new Bible. Bear-baiting was the popular sport in those pre-cinema days, and Congleton folk are still spoken of as "bears." A curiosity to be seen in the town hall is a leather belt with three bells attached, known as St. Peter's Chains. Originally worn by priests at the feast of St. Peter ad Vincula, for the last 300 years they have been used by local chimney sweeps to proclaim their annual holiday.

Third of the silk towns is Leek, over the border in Staffordshire, a place once famous for its ale. It bears the imprint typical of these edge-of-Pennine towns, the up-and-down streets, the high fortress-like mills, the clatter of clogs and the general bustle and dinginess of the smaller industrial town. Yet it has a fine Decorated church with a pinnacled tower, dedicated to Edward the Confessor, and in the yard a high carved cross believed to be Danish. Near by is a monument to William Trafford of Swythamley, who in the Civil War refused to answer any questions, merely replying "Now thus" until finally they decided he was an idiot and left him. On the stone is depicted a man threshing corn, the words "Now thus" and the date 1697.

The country round Leek has some grand scenery, for the high moorlands stretch away to the Cheshire and Derbyshire borders. The Peak District takes in a lot more of Staffordshire than most people imagine. A few miles away is Rudyard Lake, that beautiful two-mile stretch of water from which Rudyard Kipling derived his name; west of it on Biddulph Moor the people are supposed to be descended from Saracen prisoners brought back by the Crusaders. East of the lake rises Gun Moor, where the last felon in England hung in chains, and beyond it are the Roaches or Five Clouds, the most southerly of the great gritstone escarpments. Its French name of Roaches (more properly Roches) and the street in Leek called Petite France are reminders of the French prisoners who were lodged there during the Peninsular War, many of whom settled in Leek and the neighbourhood. The Roaches are in some of the wildest, loveliest, loneliest scenery in all England—I am biased, I know, for I live beside them—but honestly I do not think there is anything to compare with the wooded gorges of the Dane, and the dark forests and sheer cliffs of the Five Clouds; it is like something from Canada or Switzerland.

Leek has been called the "Capital of the Moorlands" but that title more rightfully belongs to Longnor, a village straddling the neck of land between the Manifold and the Dove; its white stone houses and little market hall cluster about the green. From the near-by village of Flash comes the slang term for counterfeit money, for in the old days the coiners had their headquarters there and "flash" money was distributed all over England. Three Shire Heads marks the boundaries of the three counties, and when challenged by a sheriff and his men the "flash-men" could escape by crossing the stream into the next county, where the writ did not run. From Flash it is a short walk to Ludchurch, which is not a church but a narrow chasm in the rocks, thirty yards deep and 300 long, a real, blown-in-the-glass Peakland wonder—but if I started telling you about the Lollards worshipping there, or how I got stuck in Lud's Cave while searching for a subterranean river, we shan't get out of Staffordshire before next Christmas.

Much of this part of Staffordshire is well over 1000 feet above sea level, hills of closely cropped herbage and clumps of trees bent toward the north-east by the prevailing winds. The population is scanty, and a mixture of dairy-farming and heifer-raising is the general occupation. The moorlanders are a frugal people, and formerly lived mainly on porridge (known as lumpy-tums, made by stirring oatmeal into boiling milk), and thin round oatcakes the size of a gramophone record baked on a "bakston." Of this region Camden wrote: "This Mooreland, so called for that it riseth higher into hils and mountaines, is a small country verily; so hard, so comfortlesse, bare, and cold, that it keepeth snow lying upon it a long while; in so much as that of a little country village named Wotton lying under Weever-hill the neighbour inhabitants have this rime rise in their mouth,

> Wooton under Wever,
> Where God came never.

From the austere beauty of the moors the River Churnet flows through rich woodlands to join the marshes by the Dove. Out of this rather dreamlike beauty rises the vast Gothic pile of Alton Towers. It was built in 1809-23 by the elder Pugin, and is said to have cost the fifteenth Earl of Shrewsbury over a million pounds. Thousands of sightseers must have been thrilled by the picturesque appearance of its rambling towers and rooms, without being one whit disturbed by the lack of composition shown in its design.

The thousand acres or so of landscape gardens were laid out by "Capability" Brown (78). Facing the mansion are the fragments of Alton Castle, built in 1175, and the chapel and convent designed by Pugin; their half-castellated, half-ecclesiastical appearance overhanging a cliff usually induces writers to speak of the "Rhineland of Staffordshire." Between Alton and Rocester are the remains of Croxden Abbey, partly incorporated in a farmhouse, a fate similar to that which overtook Dieulacres Abbey near Leek; the only public school in Staffordshire is near by at Denstone. Wooton Lodge between the Churnet and Manifold rivers is a seventeenth-century house with a front designed by Inigo Jones, while Throwley Hall nearer Ilam is a picturesque Tudor mansion which has been converted into a farmhouse.

The scenery about the Manifold is so superb that it is usually included in the Peak District, but Staffordshire might as well get the benefit (79). Above its junction with the Dove the Manifold sweeps round in a great bend whose steep, wooded banks form a magnificent amphitheatre; the place is aptly known as Paradise. In the midst of woods and gardens is Ilam church and hall (the former containing one of Chantrey's best-known sculptures), from whose windows there is a grand view of the twin pyramid-shaped peaks guarding Dovedale. Ilam's beauties are said to have suggested the idea of the Happy Valley in *Rasselas*, and here also Congreve's famous comedy *The Old Bachelor* was written. Indeed, we are in a neighbourhood with many literary associations, for at Mayfield is Tom Moore's cottage, where he wrote *Lalla Rookh* and *Those Evening Bells*. The same road brings you to Ellastone, which was the Hayslope of *Adam Bede*. A mile or so away at Wooton Hall Rousseau lived for a time while writing his *Confessions*, and in the now ruined Calwich Abbey Handel is said to have composed the *Messiah*.

Among several fine churches to be found in the wooded valleys on the edge of the moors that at Cheddleton has windows by Rossetti and Burne-Jones, and a fourteenth-century chancel with a rare medieval brass eagle on the lectern. Cheadle is a small market town whose gabled Tudor houses are gathered round the big red Catholic church which is one of Pugin's masterpieces. The altar screen, a carved oak triptych representing the Passion is the work of fifteenth-century Flemish craftsmen. Caversall church, overlooking the red walls of the seventeenth-century castle (which was built by Matthew Craddock who was one of the founders of Massachusetts), contains Chantrey's lovely figure of Lady St. Vincent. But perhaps the finest of the old churches is that at Checkley, four miles from Cheadle, which is a blending of all periods. The fourteenth-century chancel is one of the finest in

77 VIEW FROM THE TERRACE AT MAPLE HAYES,
LICHFIELD, STAFFORDSHIRE

78 A LAKE AND PAGODA, ALTON TOWERS,
STAFFORDSHIRE

79 LOOKING TO BUNSTER HILL, NEAR ILAM, STAFFORDSHIRE

Staffordshire, and contains some Flemish glass of a century earlier. In the churchyard are the shafts of three Saxon crosses. Uttoxeter (pronounced locally Uxeter), near the River Dove, is an unpretentious market town which produces agricultural machinery. A tablet in the market place commemorates the occasion when Dr. Johnson did his self-imposed penance by standing bareheaded in the rain, for refusing to tend his father's bookstall. An annual ceremony known as Penance Day is now held at Uttoxeter to commemorate this event.

Between the northern moors and the rugged uplands of Cannock Chase lies a green undulating country of low hills and slowly moving rivers. Now the Trent, having dropped 800 feet in its descent from Biddulph Moor, becomes a sober stream winding through typical dairying country. Leaving behind the dinginess of the Potteries, it flows by way of Trentham Park to the market town of Stone, where there are the scanty remains of a priory founded by Queen Ermenilda in 670. Seven miles away stands Eccleshall, whose castle was the residence of the bishops of Lichfield for over 600 years; now only a bridge and a tower remain. The church, a mixture of Early English and Perpendicular, has a fine medieval tower. This is Izaak Walton's homeland, for at Shallowford by the River Meece is the farm where he lived and the black-and-white cottage which he left to his native town of Stafford; it is now a museum and a place of pilgrimage for anglers. In the dangerous days after the battle of Worcester a friend of Walton's named George Barlow was entrusted by the Royalists with one of the Crown jewels. It was necessary to find a messenger who would carry the jewel from Barlow's home at Broughton to Charles's envoy, so Izaak Walton undertook the dangerous mission. He accomplished it successfully, though it might well have cost him his head, and resumed that tranquil, meditative life with which readers of *The Compleat Angler* are more familiar.

This borderland between Shropshire and Staffordshire is most delightful country of wooded hills and valleys and numerous streams flowing toward the Severn. Burnt Wood and Bishop's Wood are all that are left of the ancient Blore Forest. At Blore Heath was fought the second battle of the Wars of the Roses. From curiously named Talke-o'-the-Hill (though Talke itself means hill), out-of-the-way villages stretch by way of Betley, Keele, to Maer and Mucklestone. Betley parish church is a remarkable example of seventeenth-century timbering, for the clerestory, roof and nave arcades are all formed of solid tree trunks.

The county town of Staffordshire stands in pleasant wooded country by the placid River Sow. It has a history stretching back 1200 years. Once it was a walled and gated town, though these have

long since vanished, yet although largely modernised some parts
of it appear to have changed but little since Stuart times. Among
the crowded byways near St. Mary's Church are picturesque
timbered houses, of which High House in Greengate is the finest.
It is a high gabled house of four storeys and the characteristic black-
and-white appearance. Near it is the old Swan Inn, "that great
place for life and bustle" which George Borrow describes in
The Romany Rye, though Dickens thought less of it. St. Mary's was
once a collegiate church, and is one of the best of English churches
below the dignity of a minster. It is a fine cruciform building
with a transitional Norman nave, Early English chancel and south
transept, and a Decorated north transept. Near a splendid sixteenth-
century tomb and a curious altar table which was lost for 500 years
is the strangely carved white stone font in which Izaak Walton was
baptised. Stafford's other ancient church, St. Chad's, is, next to
Tutbury, the finest Norman church in the county; though restored
it appears to have changed little since the Conqueror's day.

"May the trade of Stafford be trod underfoot by all the world,"
thus Sheridan, who was M.P. for Stafford for a number of years,
epigrammatically toasted the town's leading industry, which was
then, as now, the making of boots and shoes. Stafford Castle stands
on the site of an earlier stronghold, but the present structure, which
was never finished, dates only from the beginning of the last century.

The pastoral country around Stafford contains several famous
country seats and parks, with that characteristic English blending of
beauty and comfortable living. Ingestre Hall, where King Edward
VII spent his holidays, is a reproduction of the fine Jacobean house
which was almost completely destroyed by fire last century. The
village church is believed to be one of Wren's unknown masterpieces (27). Shugborough Hall near Great Haywood is a Palladian
mansion and was once the home of Admiral Anson, who sailed
round the world and brought back a million and a half pieces-of-
eight. Wolseley Hall was the home of the Wolseleys since before
the Conquest, they having received their lands in the tenth century
for destroying wolves. Their possession of the chartered right of a
deer-leap in Cannock Chase is the only instance of its kind in
England. These places can best be reached by way of Tixall, with
its fine sixteenth-century gatehouse. But older than any of these
places are the remains of the castle at Chartley Holme, whose twelve-
foot thick walls and towers date back to the thirteenth century.
Chartley formerly possessed a herd of wild white cattle, descendants
of the aurochs domesticated by the Romans, but many of them died
of tuberculosis a few years ago and the remainder are in the Duke of
Bedford's collection at Woburn.

West of Stafford, on the road to the Shropshire border, is

Gnosall, with a fine old church that is a happy blending of Norman massiveness and Perpendicular grace. Its square tower looks down upon the green lowlands where mile-long Aqualate Mere ripples in the sun and herons stand motionless among the reeds. There is another fine Perpendicular church at Penkridge, seven miles south of Stafford, a typical small agricultural town which was more important in Saxon times than now. The church was one of the six collegiate churches in Staffordshire. The old White Hart Inn is an attractive half-timbered building. Two miles away is partly ruined Pillaton Hall, with medieval gateway, turrets and chapel overlooking the dry moat. I was told that the lord of the manor at Penkridge only sold land for railway construction on condition that the express trains halted there daily.

The wooded uplands about the little River Penk have been the setting for much romantic history. Famous houses and famous names abound, and the district is full of stories. It was to Moseley Old Hall, near Bushbury, that Charles II came after fleeing from Whiteladies and Boscobel. The place remains very much as it was when Thomas Whitegreave, the squire, hid him from the Round-heads. Colonel Carlos, who sheltered with him in that memorable oak at Boscobel, is buried in Brewood churchyard. Inside Brewood church are the painted alabaster tombs of the Giffard family, who have held Chillington Castle for 800 years and who were Counts of Longueville long before they sailed to England with the Conqueror. A wooden cross in the park marks the spot where Sir John Giffard fought and killed an escaped leopard with bow and arrow.

To the grammar school at Brewood came Samuel Johnson—not yet a doctor—seeking a post as usher, but was rejected by the headmaster because of his scarred face. When the ancient Forest of Brewood included Boscobel and Whiteladies estates Brewood was already an old, old town, its glories long departed. Among the old houses in the neighbourhood is a gabled house called Black-ladies, on the site of a Norman convent of Black Nuns. At Lapley, a mile or so to the north, there are the remains of both a Saxon and a Norman priory, or so I was informed, but when one goes collecting facts in wartime, as I did, even the most innocent questions about local buildings were apt to get you into trouble.

Between the Penk and the Trent stretch the 40,000 acres of Cannock Chase. Once a royal game preserve, very little is now left of the original forest, though its valleys with their peat-coloured streams and bracken-covered ridges with birch and pine woods are still wild enough in parts to recall the days when the region was a refuge for outlaws. For long regarded merely as a large unfertile region not worth reclaiming, in more recent times it was discovered to be rich in coal, so that now it is difficult to imagine the old town of Cannock, surrounded by coal-pits, was once a watering-place of repute. In those days Dean Swift used to stay at the Four Crosses Inn outside the town, and not liking the landlord's wife is said to have scratched the following lines on a window-pane:

> Thou fool, to hang four crosses at thy door!
> Hang up thy wife! There needs not any more.

Towns acquire fame in various ways, but Rugeley possesses the doubtful distinction of being known as the home of William Palmer, the poisoner, who murdered several persons during the last century in order to obtain their insurance money. Legend has it that when the local people petitioned Lord Palmerston to change the town's name he laughingly replied: "What do you wish to call it—Palmerstown?"

East of Rugeley, between the Trent and the Blythe, are the three Ridware villages; the name is derived from rhyd-ware or river folk. Pipe and Mavesyn Ridware take their names from former well-known families. Mavesyn Ridware church is famous for its monuments, with armoured figures of Crusaders dating from the twelfth and thirteenth centuries, and beautiful floor tiles from William the Conqueror's palace at Caen. Hamstall Ridware (Hamstall means homestead) has a Tudor manor with gatehouse and watch-tower, now a farmhouse, and an old church with some good painted glass. It is a short walk through meadows and woods to Hoar Cross, whose red stone church rising above the black-and-white cottages is one of the most beautiful modern churches in England. The widow of Meynell Ingram spent thirty-three years building it as a monument to her departed husband; certainly it is a masterpiece in stone, metal, glass and wood, preserving the essential Gothic spirit in modern dress.

All this corner of Staffordshire stretching toward the Dove is part of the ancient forest of Needwood, an area still largely rural, with dark woodlands and old black-and-white villages which cling to traditional customs. At Abbots Bromley the Horn Dance (81) takes place each September, a ritual reproduction of an old-time hunt. Twelve persons take part, six dressed to represent Robin Hood and his followers, the other six wearing reindeer horns. After dancing through the market-place the six deer men are chased by the others out of town and along the boundaries of the parish. The ceremony is believed to mark the restoration to the townsmen of certain forest rights in Henry III's time, though it may date back to a much earlier period. Until recent years the curfew was tolled here from Michaelmas to Shrove Tuesday.

Once the forest measured twenty-five miles in circumference, and contained some of the largest oaks and hollies in England. Among

80　DR. JOHNSON'S BIRTHPLACE, IN THE MARKET PLACE,
LICHFIELD, STAFFORDSHIRE

81　THE HORN DANCE AT ABBOTS BROMLEY,
STAFFORDSHIRE

82 AERIAL VIEW OF LICHFIELD CATHEDRAL, STAFFORDSHIRE

centuries-old trees were the Squitch Oak, sixty-one feet high, the Beggar's Oak, and Bagot's Walking Stick, whose trunk rose a sheer seventy feet before putting out a branch. These were contained in Bagot's Park, and now, owing to the exigencies of taxation and war most of these trees have suffered the ruthless destruction common to many of our great parklands, though it is good to know that the Walking Stick has been spared.

And so to Burton-on-Trent, which for 300 years has been famous for its ale; a red brick town criss-crossed by railway lines where enormous stacks of beer barrels proclaim its chief industry. Burton's fame rests less on its being the site of the greatest monastery in Staffordshire than on the activities of one William Bass, and his son Michael, who were fond of declaring that Nature meant Burton to brew and who obeyed this dictum to such good purpose that there are now over two dozen establishments devoted to the manufacture of liquid refreshment. As a result of these activities the Bass dynasty was able to present the town with a new bridge, town hall, drill hall, and various churches and social centres, as well as to acquire a title. But Burton had been a brewing centre long before the coming of Bass, for even in the thirteenth century the local abbots were brewing a potent beverage. At first its fame was purely local, but in the seventeenth century it was introduced to London and suited public taste so well that now Burton is the largest brewing centre in England. The fact that it was once equally famous for its alabaster industry and later for its clothing works is forgotten, while almost the entire population labours to quench the national thirst. I am not going to give astronomical figures of the number of barrels produced each year—careless talk gives away secrets—but probably you know that the presence of sulphate of lime in the local water supply is responsible for the concentration of industry here. For those interested in the academic side of thirst-quenching I will only say that our national drink is made from barley, prepared maize and sugar, boiled in hops and fermented with yeast, and that the alcoholic content varies from $2\frac{1}{2}$ to $4\frac{1}{2}$ per cent. This is considerably less than the strength of the original brew, which, when supplied to English ships trading to the Arctic, was very strong drink indeed.

But perhaps you *are* more interested in Burton Abbey than Burton beer, and at Sinai Park, two or three miles away, you will find the old summer home of the monks, now turned into a moated farmhouse.

Tutbury, an old town overlooking the Dove some miles north of Burton, has a Norman church and castle which are steeped in history. Originally a stronghold of the kings of Mercia the castle was rebuilt in William the Conqueror's day and strengthened and enlarged by John of Gaunt. The great gateway, tilt-yard, ruined house and halls are his work, but the so-called Julius Tower on the site of the vanished keep is a nineteenth-century addition. After his death the castle became Crown property and has remained so ever since. Mary Queen of Scots was imprisoned here several times, occupying a timber house in the tilt-yard, of which she wrote ". . . a walled enclosure, exposed to all the winds and inclemencies of heaven, the greater part of it rather a dungeon for base and abject criminals than for a person of my quality." Here came Charles II after his defeat at Naseby, and when the castle surrendered in 1646 the Parliamentary troops dismantled the walls so that it should never be used as a fortress again.

Tutbury church was part of the priory built by Henry de Ferrers twenty years after the Conquest. The magnificent west doorway is one of the finest examples of Norman art in England, arch within arch, all decorated with carved figures of men and animals. It is believed to be the earliest example of the use of alabaster in England. Tutbury has also an old inn and the town stocks, and was formerly known for its love of bull-baiting.

Midway between Burton and Lichfield the village of Wichnor was associated with one of the jocular tenures instituted by John of Gaunt, for the manor, like several neighbouring ones, was granted on the tenure that the holder should provide a flitch of bacon to be given to any man who could prove that he had been happily married for a year and a day. The claimant had to swear the following oath: "Hear ye, Lord of Wichnor, mayntennor and gyver of this baconne; I, A.B., sithe I wedded my wife, sithe I had her in my kepyng and at my wylle by a year and a day after our marriage, I would not have changed for none other, fairer ne fouler, richer ne poorer. And if the said B were sole and I sole, I would take her to be my wyfe before all the wymen of the world. So help me God and his saints, and all fleshes." Afterwards the happy pair were escorted back to their home on horseback, with music and singing; if the holder of the tenure refused to continue these customs he was fined a hundred shillings. Persons in the service of the Church could also claim the bacon if they had not repented of entering their profession. This counterpart of the more famous Dunmow Flitch has now fallen into disuse, but a memorial in the shape of a wooden flitch still hangs in Wichnor Lodge.

Alrewas, a mile or two away, is a village of thatched black-and-white houses gathered about a medieval church, and has long been noted for its basket-making.

The triple spires of Lichfield Cathedral (82) show far and wide above the neighbouring woods and meadows; locally they are known as the "Ladies of the Vale." The name Lichfield is said to signify "Field of the Dead" from the tradition that a thousand Christians were martyred here during the Diocletian persecutions. Lichfield stands near the centre of England, a small town in red brick whose narrow streets and occasional Elizabethan timbered houses have the atmosphere typical of a cathedral town, though now it is something of an industrial centre as well, where iron-founding, engineering and brick- and tile-making are carried on. It is a town of old inns, of antique shops, of booksellers' establish-ments, and of worthy folk of whom Dr. Johnson wrote that "they all got drunk every night and were none the worse thought of." For a place so small and out of the way (the coming of the railway deprived it of its coaching trade to Holyhead and Liverpool) it has gathered about it a cluster of famous names; it knew Johnson, Garrick, Erasmus Darwin, Joseph Addison, George Farquhar, Anna Seward (who was its literary queen), and André the spy. But most of all it is Dr. Johnson's town; the place is saturated with his personality, and owing to the corporation's tidy habit of placing inscriptions upon all buildings of literary or historical interest you can follow the career of its most illustrious son from the cradle to —well, almost to the grave. At the corner of Market Street you can see the house where he was born in 1709, now a museum. At the Three Crowns next door he and Boswell stayed, and near by is the Swan, which he also knew. You can see the house which was Dame Oliver's school, but the factory where his father manufactured parchment is now converted into cottages. Johnson's statue stands in the market-place, near Boswell's, that same market-place where people were burned alive in Mary Tudor's day (80). The Grammar School which Johnson attended, and also Garrick, Ashmole and Addison, has since been removed to a site on the outskirts of the town. There are some places of interest *not* associated with the indomitable doctor, among them being Lichfield House, a fine example of fifteenth-century timbering, and the remains of the thirteenth-century Franciscan priory now incorporated in the girls' high school. The group of fifteenth-century almshouses known as St. John's Hospital is one of the earliest examples of English archi-tecture to be built with chimneys.

Lichfield Cathedral (82) is one of the most beautiful, but by no means one of the largest, of English cathedrals, and it differs from all others by being still surmounted by three spires. It was originally founded by St. Chad, who was Bishop of Mercia in the seventh century, but of the Saxon church or of the Norman one which succeeded it nothing is left. The present building was built between 1200 and 1340 and is therefore almost entirely in the styles known as Early English and Decorated. To attempt to describe it in a paragraph or so is obviously hopeless, but a few impressions may be useful. The west front, in the exuberance of its decoration, resembles some of the Continental cathedrals. The central spire was shattered by Parliamentary cannon during the Civil War when the cathedral close was used as a royal fortress; the spire was rebuilt from a design by Wren. In the nave (7) the eye ranges from the elaborate design of the altar, a mass of marble and alabaster, to the glowing splendour of the lady chapel, whose windows are filled with glass from the ancient monastery of Herkenrode, near Liége; valued at £200 when presented to the cathedral, they are now said to be worth £15,000. The octagonal chapter house is richly carved and decorated, and in the library over it are many rare books. These include a manuscript copy of Chaucer's *Canterbury Tales* and St. Chad's copy of the Gospels. This wonderful old book was brought over from Ireland by the saint in the seventh century. Among some interesting monuments the one which is most sought after by visitors is the group known as the Sleeping Children, which established Chantrey's fame as a sculptor.

The curious "Greenhill Bower" ceremony held in Lichfield each Whit-Monday, when youths clad in chain mail parade before the city officials, is a survival of the ancient "Court of Array" when citizens used to meet for the inspection of their arms and armour.

From Lichfield it is a two-mile journey to Wall, where the remains of the Roman city of Letocetum have been scheduled as a national monument.

In the rich grazing lands adjoining Warwickshire stands Tamworth (83), above whose red roofs rises the castle first built by the Saxons in 913. Twelve hundred years of history are recorded in this ancient capital of Mercia, for deeds and charters exist dated from the royal palace at Tamworth in the eighth and ninth centuries. Even earlier is the legend of the combat here between Sir Lancelot and Sir Tarquin. Standing on an artificial mound near the junction of the Tame and Anker rivers the castle walls and keep incorporate Saxon, Norman and Tudor masonry. It is now a museum, and inside you can see coins from the castle mint, and arms and armour worn by the defenders. The church of St. Edith dates from the fourteenth century, and has a curious double staircase leading to the roof (said to be unique in England), and a crypt filled with human bones. The curious arched town hall was built by Thomas Guy, the bookseller who founded the London hospital which bears his name; he also built the seventeenth-century almshouses. The tiny chapel of St. James's Hospital, dating from 1285, is a short walk outside the town.

How many people realise that Warwickshire reaches to within a mile or so of Derbyshire? A triangle of Shakespeare's county separates Staffordshire from Leicestershire, a green undulating

83 TAMWORTH CHURCH ABOVE THE TOWN ROOFS,
STAFFORDSHIRE

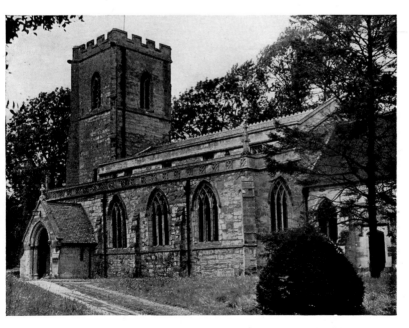

84 THE FOURTEENTH-CENTURY CHURCH,
WOLVEY, WARWICKSHIRE

86 THE CENTRAL FEATURE OF THE
SOUTH FRONT

85 THE ALABASTER HALL

landscape whose pleasant valleys and wooded parklands are being marred by brick villas and coalpits (though some of the pits have been worked since the fourteenth century). Secluded old-world villages remain tucked away in the byways, such as Astley with its castle which is really a fortified manor house, and Lea Marston, where Lord Norton framed the first constitution for New Zealand. Curdworth church is largely Norman, with a fifteenth-century tower. Mancetter, once a Roman station, has a quaint manor house of the fifteenth century. But the place which appeals most to me is Meriden, perhaps because it claims to be the centre of England. Though I have passed through it a score of times I still keep a sharp lookout for the war memorial erected by the Cyclists' Touring Club and the old church with its carved oak alms chest and chained copy of Jewel's *Apology* of 1609.

The market town of the area is Atherstone, which is not much of a place though it gives its name to a hunt; the twelfth-century church was rebuilt in 1849 except for the tower and chancel. I was told that Henry VII received the sacrament there before the battle of Bosworth. In the neighbouring town of Nuneaton the making of bricks and tiles appears to be the main preoccupation of the inhabitants. The town is mainly Late Industrial, though there is a sixteenth-century grammar school and a couple of old churches. At Chilvers Coton, now a suburb, was born Mary Ann Evans, better known as George Eliot. Most of the district round here can be found described in one or another of her novels; Chilvers Coton was Shepperton and Nuneaton was Milby. Nothing remains of the nunnery founded by Gervase Paynel, except the church which was rebuilt in 1236 and "restored" some 600 years later.

Among other monastic remains in the locality the gate-chapel of Merevale Abbey, near Atherstone, has become the parish church, while the Norman gatehouse and conventual church at Polesworth contains the only effigy of an abbess in England. Maxstoke is better known for its castle than for its fourteenth-century priory, now converted into a farmhouse. Alvecote Priory is also incorporated in a farmhouse. A pleasing place with the remains of a castle is Hartshill, where the poet Michael Drayton was born in 1563, and at Coleshill there are also some pleasant eighteenth-century houses and a church with one of the most beautiful spires in the county. A place with an exciting history is the old hall at Caldecote, on the Leicestershire border, where eight men held the house against Prince Rupert and fought until they had to melt down pewter mugs and dishes to make bullets.

LOWLAND AND WOLD

South of the Trent, beyond the Staffordshire border, Midland England is a region of undulating grasslands and fat and lazy rivers. It is field and hedge country, as typically English as a Constable landscape.

> A land of covert, copse and quiet waters,
> Where men of deathless name have walked.

Enge-land, the meadow-land, the Saxons and the Danes called it, when they drove the prows of their ships ashore and saw before them, not eternal rocks and fir trees, but the verdant grass plains around the Trent, so England it became. Leicestershire shares with Rutland and Northants the most famous hunting country in England—the Shires; to the red-coated huntsmen who follow the hounds over its wonderful greenness it is the principal portion of England, the remaining part being merely "the Provinces." It has been described as "the prose of English landscape; prose with rare man-making, Empire-making qualities."

This typically English landscape stretches north and south along the Trent, as from Burton of ale-making fame that lordly stream flows through pleasantly wooded farming country to Nottingham. North of the river the villages of Sudbury, Marston Montgomery, Brailsford and Shirley are finely situated. Nearer Derby is Kedleston Hall (86), an eighteenth-century mansion which Dr. Johnson declared would do excellently for a big town hall. Despite this gibe it is a fine building in the Classical style, whose dimensions and splendour of decoration are surpassed by few halls in England. The great hall is one of the most magnificent rooms to be found anywhere (85). The interior decorations and furniture were designed by the Adam brothers.

South of the Trent is Repton, an old capital of Mercia, and here the first cathedral church in the kingdom was built, and the first bishop buried here as long ago as 656. It is a pleasant little place, a mingling of old and new buildings grouped round an old market cross with high steps. The grammar school was founded by Sir John Port in 1556, and is approached by a delightful old priory gateway belonging to an establishment of Black Canons founded four centuries earlier; the refectory now serves as a schoolroom. The church of St. Wystan is noted for its fine spire and its Saxon crypt (88).

From Repton the river flows on through gently undulating hills, past old churches and older burial grounds. Anchor Church near Foremark Hall is a group of caves said to have been cut out of the rock by a hermit. Swarkeston Bridge, which carries the main road south from Derby, was the furthest point south reached by Prince Charlie's Highlanders in 1745. Local legend has it that the bridge was built by two sisters whose lovers were drowned while crossing the Trent. A little to the north is Chellaston, from whose famous quarries came the alabaster for carving the effigies on church tombs.

The little boot and hosiery town of Melbourne is noted for its old cathedral-like church and the fact that it was the birthplace of Thomas Cook, that patron saint of tourists. Melbourne Hall has sixteen acres of Dutch gardens and a celebrated yew avenue. Through its connection with Lord Melbourne the town gave its name to the capital of Victoria, Australia. Three miles away, in

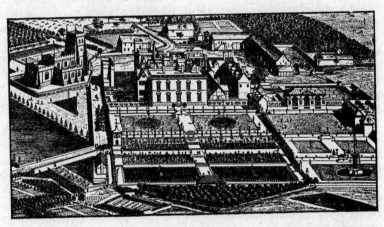

[*Engraved by J. Kip, 1724*

THE CHURCH AND MANOR HOUSE, STAUNTON HAROLD, LEICESTERSHIRE

Leicestershire, the isolated limestone mass of Breedon Hill rises abruptly from the green farmlands, its summit crowned by an old church. Do not confuse it with that Bredon Hill in Worcestershire of which Housman wrote: "In summer time to Bredon, my love and I did go." The old church stands inside a prehistoric fortress known as the Bulwarks, and contains a remarkable treasure in the shape of a Saxon stone frieze built into the walls; if put together its total length would measure about eighty feet. The carvings of birds, animals, human figures, foliage and scrollwork are unique in England, and surpass any other eighth- or ninth-century Saxon work in Europe. They are an astonishing thing to find in a remote Midland village, and some authorities believe them to have been brought here from the Continent. But how did they get here?

Breedon village at the foot of the hill has a round eighteenth-century lock-up with conical roof and iron-studded door.

A couple of miles along the same road brings you to Staunton Harold (85), a mansion deriving its name from a Saxon owner before the Conquest. It is a huge red-brick house dating mostly from about 1770, with a chapel as large as many a village church. The north-east or library front is said to be the work of Inigo Jones. The church is one of the finest in Leicestershire and is remarkable as being one of the few churches built in the days of the Commonwealth (90). It was built in the Perpendicular style in 1653 by Sir Robert Shirley "when all things sacred were throughout the nation either demolished or profaned." "Well, if you have money to build a church then you can afford to build a warship too," Cromwell remarked dryly. Sir Robert was compelled to comply with the demand, but it did not save him from dying in the Tower at the early age of twenty-eight. The church is a rather overwhelming place, with a sumptuous interior full of marble, ironwork and oak panelling; the wooden ceiling is painted to represent the sky, there is magnificent purple velvet upholstery, but the finest thing of all is the later iron screen in the chancel, made by Robert Bakewell.

Collieries, potteries and brickworks stretch along the Warwickshire-Leicestershire boundary, and Ashby-de-la-Zouch lies in the middle of a coalfield. Readers of *Ivanhoe* will recall the romantic episodes which took place at Ashby, though the truth is that Sir Walter Scott invented them all. At Smisby, a mile or so outside the town, is the tournament ground where Ivanhoe defeated the Black Knight; once it really was one of the most famous tilting-grounds in England, now it is just open meadows. But the castle still stands, and the old church of St. Helen, and a nineteenth-century manor house, all grouped together at the top of the town. The castle is a somewhat battered affair, but its great tower and hall, chapel and kitchens retain something of the atmosphere of a fifteenth-century fortress. Of course Mary Queen of Scots was imprisoned here (only for a night) and James I and his queen were entertained here in 1603. After being besieged for eight months during the Civil War the castle suffered the usual fate of Royalist strongholds; it was dismantled.

The 500-year-old church contains some interesting memorials, and a curious finger pillory, used for punishing those who misbehaved themselves in church. Supported on two posts a yard high is a horizontal beam containing a series of grooves into which the disorderly person's fingers were thrust; when another hinged beam was locked into position on top it must have been very uncomfortable. Ashby once hoped to acquire fame as a spa, using saline waters brought from Moira Colliery, but the venture failed.

87   MELBOURNE CHURCH, DERBYSHIRE

88   THE SAXON CRYPT, REPTON CHURCH, DERBYSHIRE

90 THE WEST ENTRANCE, STAUNTON
HAROLD CHURCH, LEICESTERSHIRE.

89 THE DECORATED ARCADE, STOKE
GOLDING CHURCH, LEICESTERSHIRE

Three miles eastward is Coleorton Hall, whose owners are one of the few English families who can really trace their family history back to the Norman Conquest. The present building is a handsome nineteenth-century house in the Classical style. It is rich in literary and artistic associations, for Sir George Beaumont (who was one of the founders of the National Gallery), delighted in the society of writers and artists. Here came Byron, Scott, Southey, while to Wordsworth it was almost a second home.

Among the green meadowlands near the little town of Market Bosworth was fought the battle of Bosworth Field, which, thanks to the genius of Shakespeare, bulks larger in popular imagination than many a bloodier and more recent conflict. Here in 1485 Richard II was defeated and killed by the Earl of Richmond, who was crowned king on the battlefield. Crown Hill is, by tradition, the spot where this happened. At the local grammar school young Samuel Johnson, fresh from Oxford, acted as second master or usher for some months, and hated every minute of it. Johnson's name is also linked with the neighbouring hamlet of Appleby Parva, for he tried to obtain the mastership of the red-brick grammar school, but failed. Incidentally, this is the only school known to have been built by Wren.

The name Barton-in-the-Beans recalls the old saying: "Shake a Leicestershire man by the collar, and you will hear the beans rattling in his belly." Leicestershire folk were always partial to beans, which grew luxuriantly here and were used as food for man and beast. Of curiously named Hog's Norton (which more delicately minded people refer to as Norton-Juxta-Twycross) there is a libellous saying that "even the pigs snore in Hog's Norton." Near by is Gopsall Hall, an imposing Classical structure where Handel is supposed to have written part of the *Messiah*.

This same district of south-west Leicestershire has associations with two of the greatest names in English religious history, for at Fenny Drayton was born George Fox, the founder of the Society of Friends, and at Lutterworth John Wycliffe was rector for nineteen years. George Fox's timber-framed cottage has been shipped to the United States, and an obelisk in the main street is his only memorial. He believed that God is in every man and spoke to every man direct; because he was opposed to established churches, paid clergy, military service and capital punishment he was eight times imprisoned and frequently beaten and stoned. Although John Wycliffe preached strongly against the veneration of relics, the church at Lutterworth contains various articles traditionally associated with him, and the sightseer can examine a chair, part of an embroidered vestment, the pulpit, and a refectory table, whose authenticity appears to be extremely doubtful. But it cannot show his burial place, for twenty-five years after his death his bones were dug up by the Pope's instructions and burned. The church dates from the twelfth century, but most of the earlier work has vanished, though there are some interesting medieval mural paintings, somewhat over-restored.

Of other stories which I collected while visiting this area, surely the most curious must be that concerning William Staresmore, the eccentric parson of Swinford, in the Avon Valley. I was told that he had a fine orchard of fruit trees, and to prevent the apples being stolen used to chain a dog to each one. He had strict ideas about the time for going to bed at night, and used to lock the servants in the house each evening to make sure they didn't get into mischief. One morning he got up early to release the dogs from their apple trees, and they got so excited they chased him into the pond—there were fifty-eight of them!—and as the servants were locked in the house they couldn't help him. So that was the end of William Staresmore.

At Husband's Bosworth in 1616 nine women were charged with having bewitched a boy, and were burned as witches. As the boy still continued to have fits six more women were sentenced to death and not until it was proved that he was an epileptic were they reprieved.

The undulating pastures south of Leicester form part of the central watershed of England, for of the streams which rise here some flow toward the Avon and the Irish Sea, others to the Welland and the Wash, while those flowing north join the Soar and the Trent. Once this region had a much greater population than now, and cottages and smallholdings thronged where now the grasslands spread, but the early enclosures swept them all away. This depopulation of the countryside was foreseen as early as Queen Elizabeth's reign when a local rector named John Moore published a pamphlet in which enclosure "which doth unpeople townes and uncorne fields, is arraigned, convicted, and condemned." Hinckley, the third-largest town in the county, is an industrial and market town with a restored Gothic church of St. Mary.

How different from the grasslands is the upland region of Charn-wood Forest (92). Geologically there is nothing quite like it anywhere in England. It is less a forest than a range of rugged granite hills, and has been described as a piece of Wales which has been taken up and set down in the green heart of Leicestershire. Certainly this is not a bad description, for though none of its summits reach a thousand feet it has all the characteristics of a mountain range in miniature; here you will find rocky gorges, hills crowned by spectacular crags, dark lakes and woods, and vast expanses of heath and bracken. Geologists have described it as a piece of buried

Triassic landscape, whose crags were polished by the hot winds when Leicestershire was a sandswept desert. Once it formed part of the great Forest of Arden, which in Roman times extended from the Avon to the Trent. In Saxon times it was a hunting-ground and was so extensive that a squirrel might hop six miles from tree to tree without touching the ground. Now there is more open land than forest, for during the great enclosures of the nineteenth century much of it was made into parks and farmlands.

Five miles west of Leicester is Bradgate Park (92), which contains the ruins of the home of that ill-fated girl who was for nine days Queen of England—Lady Jane Grey. The 18,000 acres of Charnwood were divided amongst various manors and religious establishments, of which the names only survive in several cases, but for over 700 years there has been a deer park at Bradgate and herds of red and fallow deer have trooped among the oaks. Bradgate might well have gone the way of many old estates and been broken up to suit the purposes of the speculative builder, had not Charles Bunnion in 1928 purchased it from the Greys of Groby and presented it to Leicester "that for all time it might be preserved in its natural state." Altogether there are over 1200 acres of natural forest scenery.

Bradgate is usually reached by way of Newton Linford, a quaint old place of thatched cottages and a somewhat over-restored medieval church. The Gothic memorial window to Lady Jane Grey was placed there in 1915. The ruins of the moated red-brick mansion which was her birthplace stand on a low ridge looking toward Cropston Reservoir, whose intense blue colour makes it appear a natural lake. Bradgate was begun by the first Marquis of Dorset in the last years of the fifteenth century, and is one of the earliest unfortified houses to be built in England, and one of the first of the great houses to be built of brick. Four towers more or less complete, the chapel with its alabaster tomb of the founder, part of the kitchens, and sundry walls and fragments, help to give some idea of the appearance of the early Tudor mansion.

The old mulberry tree hanging over the wall of the kitchen garden is believed to be one of the seven brought to England by Sir Walter Raleigh early in the seventeenth century. The surrounding woods contain other fine trees, including a fine avenue of Spanish chestnuts, and some magnificent cedars of Lebanon which were planted a hundred years ago. Most curious of all are the pollard oaks, which, so legend tells us, were chopped off by the foresters on the day that the young queen was beheaded.

It was in one of the towers that Roger Ascham found Lady Jane Grey reading Plato's *Phaedo* while the rest of the family were out hunting. She was then thirteen, and four years later she was to die at the Tower. During the Civil War Bradgate was captured by Prince Rupert in 1642, and early the following century it was damaged by fire and abandoned. A curious story relates that it was burned down by the Countess of Stamford because she did not like living there. Since then the only event worth chronicling was the shooting by the Earl of Stamford and some friends of 4949 head of game in the park in two days.

Adjoining the park is Swithland Wood where old slate pits present a weirdly impressive sight. Ringed round by sheer cliffs dropping to the dark blue water the pits might be old crater lakes. The cutting of Swithland slates was once a prosperous local industry, and for over a hundred years a school of tombstone carvers flourished in Leicester. The quarries were finally closed about 1860, and now the dark blue slates are in such demand that people buy old cottages in order to strip their roofs. A coarser slate was worked much later at Groby, but it was Swithland slates by which Leicestershire is best known, for they cover the roofs of nearly all the ancient buildings in the county.

Groby Pool is a picturesque pond of forty acres, and is a favourite haunt of wild fowl. The local proverbs "To thatch Groby Pool with pancakes" meant that a task was impossible, while "For his death there is many a wet eye in Groby Pool" signified that no tears were shed at his death.

South of Groby the great square tower and gatehouse of Kirby Muxloe Castle rise above the wide moat; actually the place is not a castle but a fortified manor house of the fifteenth century. It is a fine example of medieval brickwork, for Lord Hastings who started building it in 1481 employed the same mason who built the brick castle at Tattershall in Lincolnshire. The house was never finished, owing to its owner being beheaded, and now the ruined bastions and roofless hall above the barrel-vaulted entrance are in the care of the Office of Works. From this turreted gateway the luckless Lord Hastings went to that memorable scene in which Richard II cries, *à la* Shakespeare:

> Off with his head! Now by St. Paul I swear
> I will not dine until I see the same.

In a secluded valley in the heart of the forest are the ruins of Ulverscroft Priory, the finest ecclesiastical remains in Leicestershire. Little is left of the original Augustinian priory founded about 1134, but incorporated in farm buildings are parts of the prior's lodging, a refectory with reader's pulpit, a guest house (now a barn) and other relics of a fourteenth-century monastic establishment. Above the moat rises the lofty tower of the priory church containing cells used by the recluses of the order. How the community met its end is not

92 BRADGATE PARK, CHARNWOOD FOREST,
LEICESTERSHIRE

91 WOODHOUSE EAVES CHURCH IN
CHARNWOOD FOREST, LEICESTERSHIRE

93 KINGS MILL, CASTLE DONINGTON, ON THE
RIVER TRENT, LEICESTERSHIRE

94 THE PACKHORSE BRIDGE, ANSTY,
LEICESTERSHIRE

known, but superstitious folk are shown a peculiar stain on the floor of the prior's lodging, which, it is said, no amount of scrubbing will remove.

Of the nunnery of Grace Dieu near Whitwick little is left but the fragments of two towers and the walls of the chapel, but a mile or so away stand the splendid buildings of the new Abbey of Mt. St. Bernard. Founded in 1835, this modern Cistercian monastery was the first Roman Catholic religious house to be built in England since the Reformation. In the midst of what was formerly a desert of grey rock rise the church and cloisters, chapter house, library, refectory and guest-house, so that, quite literally, the monks may be said to have made the wilderness blossom like a rose. Among the granite peaks of Charnwood some seventy monks employ themselves in farming and useful trades, even to tailoring and gasmaking. The church was designed by the elder Pugin, in the severe undecorated Gothic traditional of the order; it was completed at Pentecost, 1939. "It is to be consecrated when Hitler dies," laughingly remarked the monk who showed me round.

It is erroneously believed that the greater portion of Charnwood Forest is closed to the public. In Mr. J. B. Firth's *Highways and Byways in Leicestershire* there are several statements which have given rise to the idea that the public are entirely excluded. It is true that when the forest was enclosed good roads were provided but no provision was made for public footpaths, but this mistake has been rectified to a considerable extent. As well as Bradgate Park and Swithland Wood, already mentioned, Bardon Hill, 912 feet, the highest point in the county, and Old John and Windmill Hills are accessible by footpath. Personally I had no difficulty in going where I wished; but perhaps that is the typical English way—the public have no rights but go everywhere.

The western fringe of the forest is dotted with colliery villages (a name like Coalville tells its own story), but northward the grasslands sweep on to Derbyshire. On a steep sandstone ridge overlooking the Trent is Castle Donington (93), whose high-banked gardens of the old cottages by the church are part of the moat and foundations of the vanished stronghold. The church is chiefly Early English work, and contains some curious monuments, the oldest being a tonsured figure sculptured in stone, dating from 1320. The spire is a landmark for miles around. Two miles away is Donington Hall, once a place of refuge for King Charles X of France, and during the 1914–18 war an internment camp for German officers; you can see a tunnel through which a couple of them escaped. The present hall was built in 1795 by William Wilkins, the architect of the National Gallery, in the fashionable style known as Strawberry Hill Gothic. As it was destined later to become a hotel and "show place," perhaps he designed better than he realised. The deer park with its magnificent trees has become a motor-racing track and exhaust fumes enshroud old Chaucer's Oak, which was forty-four feet round when Evelyn wrote about it in his *Sylva*. I wonder what Tom Moore, who wrote some of his *Irish Melodies* here, would think, or that eminent lady who founded the Countess of Huntingdon's Connection, whose home it was?

From near-by Lockington come stories of that sporting parson Robert Story, who had a passion for the unlawful sport of cock-fighting, which sometimes took place in the church itself. He and his friends were matching birds one day when the place was raided by the police. Story managed to escape, and next day in his capacity as magistrate solemnly fined all his friends for breaking the law! At both Lockington and Castle Donington the curfew was rung nightly in winter at eight o'clock.

North of the eighteenth-century bridge across the Trent at Shardlow stands Elvaston Castle, more Strawberry Hill Gothic, where great iron gates from a palace in Madrid lead through won-derful evergreen glades and flower gardens to an artificial lake with rocky shores and islands; many of the trees were transplanted full-grown from long distances. Across the Derwent, an hour's walk away, is Dale Abbey, a fascinating place. Here are the ruins of an early thirteenth-century Premonstratensian house. Measuring barely twenty-five feet square, the tiny church of All Saints is itself really two churches made into one, and shares the same roof with a half-timbered farmhouse; for some time the place was used as a public-house, the vestry being the bar.

Dale is on the edge of that long, narrow belt of industrialism which stretches along the Derbyshire-Nottinghamshire boundary, where ironworks, collieries and hosiery factories occupy the country between Chesterfield, Clay Cross, Alfreton, Heanor and Ilkeston. At its southern extremity is Long Eaton, a town once known for its lace-making but now perhaps better known on account of its proximity to the famous Trent College. Beyond the sombre Erewash the farmlands are gradually being swallowed up by Nottingham and its industrial outposts, which may soon spell doom to old villages like Bramcote and Attenborough. Attenborough has the house where Cromwell's son-in-law lived, that "Damn'd remonstring Henry Ireton," as the Cavaliers called him, the man who signed the death-warrant of Charles I. Facing it across the Trent is Barton-in-Fabis, where a curious old custom persists; each year a huge open field is divided among the local tenants in units known as "gates," each "gate" being rather less than two acres.

Below Long Eaton the River Soar flows northward through the red sandstone hills to join the Trent. The Soar is the chief river of

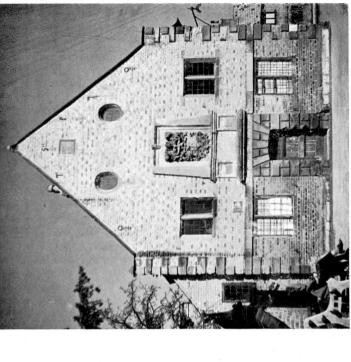

95 MEMORIAL TO SIR THOMAS PARKYNS (1663–1741) IN THE CHURCH. DESIGNED BY HIMSELF AND MADE DURING HIS LIFETIME

96 SIR THOMAS PARKYNS HOSPITAL AND SCHOOL

BUNNY, NOTTINGHAMSHIRE

97 LATE SEVENTEENTH-CENTURY HOUSE AT
KIBWORTH, LEICESTERSHIRE

98 THE LATE EIGHTEENTH-CENTURY VICARAGE AT
CHURCH LANGTON, LEICESTERSHIRE, IN THE ADAM STYLE

Leicestershire, and divides the county into two almost equal halves, each with its characteristic scenery; westward is the granite country of Charnwood, eastward the grassy uplands known as the Wolds. The river rises on the central watershed inside the Warwickshire boundary, and having collected the waters of the Rothley, the Fishpool and other streams, becomes at Loughborough a navigable stream and the boundary with Nottinghamshire. Of the various Nottinghamshire villages hidden among winding lanes by the Soar perhaps none is more quaint than Sutton Bonington, which has gabled old houses, half timber, half stone, one with the intriguing name of Hobgoblins. Another cottage has an outline like a big letter A, showing the same type of cruck construction of the better-known Tea-pot Hall at Scrivelsby, in Lincolnshire.

Among neighbouring villages East Leake church has the distinction of possessing a shawm, a big tin trumpet about eight feet long, which was used till 1855 for vamping the bass. "With trumpets also and shawms" they formerly made joyful noises unto the Lord, but now only half a dozen remain in England. Not far away the commonplace village of Gotham was celebrated for its so-called Merry Tales, telling how the Mad Men of Gotham dragged a cart to the top of a barn to shade the roof from the sun, burnt down a forge to get rid of a wasps' nest, tried to drown an eel in a pond, and performed other foolish acts. But it is for building a hedge round the cuckoo to keep it from flying away that the place is best known, and they will still point out to you the Cuckoo Bush where this exploit is supposed to have taken place. Folklorists have waged wordy warfare over the origin of these curious stories, but local tradition declares that the inhabitants did not want King John to build a hunting lodge there, or make a public road across their meadows, so they pretended to act foolishly in order to encourage him to go elsewhere. Believe it or not!

Another place of interest near by is Bunny, which has nothing to do with rabbits, but signifies a marshy place. It is a warm, red-brick village with a Decorated church (with a beautiful chancel), houses, barns, and an old school (96) and almshouses. Motorists may recall Bunny Hill which evoked curses from coach and car drivers in the old days. Bunny Hall was aptly known as Crazy Hall, for brick, stone and stucco are blended together in curious fashion, with a tall brick tower stuck up on top. It was the home of that seventeenth-century Nottinghamshire oddity, Sir Thomas Parkyns (95), who preferred to be known as the Wrestling Baronet. The annual wrestling match which he established in the village was kept going for over ninety years, the prize being a gold-laced hat. Two wrestlers were kept at the hall to train the young men of the village, and any promising young sportsman could come and tackle the

NMC : N

baronet on his own dining-room carpet. He wrote a book on the Cornish style of wrestling, also a Latin grammar, and was fond of displaying Latin quotations about his estate. Yet he was a good magistrate and landowner, improved the church and farmhouses, and built a free school and almshouses. At a time when a magistrate could order any man, except a blacksmith, to do harvest work, he tried to start an organisation for the payment of better wages, and his proposed ninepence a day for farmworkers was a great advance. He was fond of collecting stone coffins, which he gave away to anybody who wanted one; he is buried in one.

This is a long way from the River Soar, and there is no space to tell of the other things in the church, or of the many other churches and halls in the neighbourhood.

So, back to the river, and with hardly a look at Kegworth, where Tom Moore lived at The Cedars while writing his *Melodies* (when he wasn't gallivanting about with his more aristocratic acquaintances), south to Dishley Grange where lived an eighteenth-century worthy who did as much for England as any of the great engineers or explorers. Here lived Robert Bakewell whose genius as a breeder of sheep and cattle provided the food for the rapidly expanding populations of the new industrial centres and without which the work of the great inventors and engineers could never have materialised. He started the new-fangled idea of irrigation, and surrounded the fields of his model farm with canals, and spent a great portion of his seventy years travelling round the country examining stock, evolving new breeds out of old nondescript types. He established the science of pedigree stock-breeding, becoming the greatest pioneer of agricultural science in the world. The sixteen shillings stud-fee which he charged for hiring out his first rams for the season increased until it rose to 800 and then 1200 guineas. Now most of the stock in England shows the effects of his years of effort. To Dishley Grange came visitors of high and low degree from all over Europe, to learn about his discoveries. Yet his country appreciated him so little that twice he nearly went bankrupt, and had to be helped by his friends.

Loughborough is the second-biggest town in the county, but it is not a particularly interesting place apart from its bell-foundry. Of the villages strewn along the Soar Valley Mountsorrel appears to be quarrying itself away and Barrow-on-Soar's fame rests on the Ichthyolithi or huge fossil fish dug up there. Rothley Temple is an Elizabethan mansion incorporating part of the old religious house of the Knights Templars, with their thirteenth-century chapel adjoining; if you know your Macaulay you may also know that this was his birthplace. But did you know that at Thurcaston, a couple of miles away, was born that outspoken Englishman, bishop and

99   THE QUORN AT BEEBY

100   THE BELVOIR PASSING THROUGH BOTTESFORD

LEICESTERSHIRE HUNTING SCENES

[From a painting by John Ferneley, c. 1828

101   THE FERNELEY FAMILY PEW IN MELTON MOWBRAY
CHURCH, LEICESTERSHIRE

preacher, Hugh Latimer, who was one of the 300 persons burned by Mary Tudor in the name of Christianity? An old timbered house is pointed out as his birthplace, though it is more than likely that the original farmhouse disappeared long ago. But in the little church with the high-pitched roof and rare wooden screen there is a marble tablet dedicated to "The great champion of the Protestant faith."

The Wolds begin east of the Soar and stretch for nearly twenty miles to the Vale of Belvoir, where a second and higher range sweeps southward along the Rutland border to Market Harborough in the valley of the Welland. This is part of the oolite belt which runs through the Cotswolds, Northamptonshire and Rutland into Lincolnshire. The marlstone and limestone provide attractive building material as can be seen in the many fine churches and country houses which are a feature of the district. At Wistow, Rolleston and Newton Harcourt are fine Elizabethan mansions, but perhaps the best Elizabethan house in the county is Carlton Curlieu, though the gabled Dutch front was added in the seventeenth century. Neville Holt, that rambling fifteenth-century mansion stuck on a hilltop, has been described as "the most picturesque house in the Shire." Thomas Palmer's oriel, dated 1476, is a gem; the house is now used as a preparatory school for Uppingham. Noseley Hall, the ancestral seat of the Hazleriggs for over 500 years, is an unpretentious eighteenth-century building, but the chantry chapel adjoining it was once a collegiate church and has a beautiful interior. Tradition declares that the oak panelling in the chancel came from the *Mayflower*. Every hilltop in this green countryside seems to have its spire or tower, but Wigston Magna is popularly known as Wigston Two Steeples, because it is distinguished by having two churches.

A dozen miles south-east of Leicester is the little industrial and fox-hunting centre of Market Harborough (21), in rich grazing country beside the infant Welland. It is a pleasant red-brick town and is to the Billesden and Fernie Hunts what Melton Mowbray is to the Quorn; Whyte-Melville's rambling novel *Market Harborough* depicts the life of the hunting fraternity who thronged its streets and lanes. Otherwise nothing very exciting seems to have happened since the battle of Naseby, when King Charles held a hurried council of war in the town and then rode out to fight his last battle. If the big red corset factory fails to arouse your admiration there is a fine Perpendicular church dedicated to St. Dionysius (p. 97) (its founding is wrongly attributed to John of Gaunt, as an act of atonement for his illicit attachment to Cathrene Swinford), but the interior fails to fulfil the expectations aroused by its lofty octagonal crocketed spire. Perhaps the quaintest thing in the town is the seventeenth-century grammar school "on stilts," with butter market below (10), a half-timbered structure with gabled walls and ornamental bargeboards. Both school and market have now been shifted elsewhere.

Adjoining Market Harborough are the Bowdens, Great and Small, with their thatched cottages and spacious green. Great Bowden Church has a wall painting of the Last Judgment. The five Langton villages crown a low range of hills. Church Langton has one of the finest churches in the county, built probably between 1320 and 1347, though the tower was added a century later. The magnificent clerestoried interior was restored in the eighteenth century by William Hanbury, who utilised his love of music and of trees to raise money to beautify the church and village. He rightly declared that to neglect arboriculture was a serious national loss and believed that a scientifically conducted system of tree-planting could be made to yield substantial profits. He planted trees everywhere in the neighbourhood, and the future justified his enterprise, for the income derived from them helped to make the village one of the most charming in Leicestershire. Near the church is a super-rectory, a mellow red-brick Georgian house designed by Robert Adam (98).

Hallaton, that rambling village which Leland described as "a pretty tounlet," is known less for the charm of its thatched cottages, stone houses and church with thirteenth-century spire (103), than for its curious old customs of "Hare Pie Scrambling" and "Bottle Kicking" which are observed annually on Easter Monday. The rector holds part of the parish land on condition that he provides two meat pies, two small casks of ale, and two dozen penny loaves to be scrambled for by the local inhabitants. The ceremony takes place at Hare Pie Bank, and the resulting struggle, is a rougher version of the pancake tossing at Westminster School. When one rector refused to provide the pies the village was placarded with signs "No pie, no parson." In the "Bottle Kicking" a bottle of ale is kicked about the village by teams from Hallaton and neighbouring Medbourne, the goal being to get it across the local brook. The winning team must get two out of three bottles, and it is a firm tradition that Hallaton must win; afterwards the foaming ale is drunk by the players. To punish one local resident who protested against "keeping up these forgotten pagan customs" the players diverted the course of the game to his front lawn and flower beds, and left them looking as though a battle had been fought there.

Medbourne stands on the site of a Roman villa; it also claims a manor house dating from the thirteenth century, and a perfect specimen of an old packhorse bridge. Incidentally, it is recorded of a former rector that, asked one day to pray for rain, he replied:

[*Drawn by J. Johnson, F.S.A.*

ST. DIONYSIUS' CHURCH, MARKET HARBOROUGH,
LEICESTERSHIRE

"All right. I'll pray for it. But it's no damned good with the wind in this quarter."

This is hunting country (99), and most of the place-names are associated with the sport. Much as I love the austere beauty of the high moors I must confess to a sneaking admiration for the hedge and coppice country. There is little mystery about the high Pennine ridges, whose miles-long slopes are so free and open that all the world can see what is happening there. Sometimes I feel an urge for a less spacious, more intimate type of scenery, a land of little winding rivers and jungle-like valleys where you can never see very far ahead, and where there is mystery.

Now your opinion of fox-hunting may range from Oscar Wilde's comment on the English gentleman galloping after a fox—"the unspeakable in full pursuit of the uneatable"—to the *Encyclopedia Brittanica*'s definition that "resorted to as a recreation the practice of the chase indicates a considerable degree of civilisation, and some-times ultimately becomes the almost distinctive employment of the classes which are possessed of the most leisure and wealth." But the hunting-folk do add a touch of the picturesque which England can ill afford to lose, and he whose pulse does not quicken at the sound of a hunting-horn or the sight of a red coat must be a very poor-spirited fellow indeed. And I must confess to a sneaking regard for the fox, even though one got away with eight of our best laying hens a month or so back and cost me several pounds. He is the only beautiful wild thing left in England with guts enough to challenge the "superiority" of the human race. But perhaps such sentiments are not really suited to a land worker whose present concern is the regeneration of British agriculture. Whether we could afford to maintain foxes and hunting if England was adequately farmed is a debatable question. At the moment feeling about raids by foxes in our Cheshire hills has resulted in a war of extermination; within seven miles of the farm dozens of foxes were trapped or shot last winter, twenty within a fortnight. Of course this has not been done without protests from certain gentry that "shooting a fox is impossible," but leaving aside A. P. Herbert's

> There are some things that are not done,
> To shoot a fox, of course, is one.

why is such an act considered "impossible"? Up here in the hills foxes have been shot from times immemorial, and in neighbouring Pennine valleys where hounds have never been kept the hunting of the fox with firearms has always been a recognised sport.

But hunting country is more than mere landscape; the human qualities and associations appeal as strongly. The history of the sport is told in various volumes but to discover the authentic

102 MELTON MOWBRAY, LEICESTERSHIRE

103 THE VILLAGE OF HALLATON, LEICESTERSHIRE

104   THE CHURCH AND OLD HALL, RAGDALE,
LEICESTERSHIRE

105   THE FOURTEENTH-CENTURY INTERIOR OF
GADDESBY CHURCH, LEICESTERSHIRE

flavour go to Melton Mowbray (102), which is the "capital" of fox-hunting Leicestershire. Capital, that is, by consensus of opinion, as well as by royal patronage. Melton lives by hunting and as soon as the Quorn have met at Kirkby Gate on the first Monday in November it wakes from its summer sleep and thenceforward its streets will be ever echoing the clatter of hooves and conversations will concern little else but horses, hounds and foxes. "A quaint, old-world sporting town " is its usual description, though curiously enough it does not house the headquarters of any hunt. Out of the season it is just a commonplace town, busy only on market days, when its talk is of Stilton cheese and pork pies. It has a fine church, an old Bede House built in 1640 and now a museum, and another house reputed to have belonged to Anne of Cleves after her lucky escape from marrying Henry VIII.

Leicestershire men acclaim Melton church as the most beautiful parish church in England (101); certainly it is one of the finest in a county of fine churches. It has been described as a cathedral in miniature, cruciform in shape, with a high central tower. Begun in the thirteenth century, it is a blending of all styles; the most prominent feature is the magnificent clerestory of forty-eight windows, added early in the sixteenth century. The 600-year-old Galilee porch was formerly used for housing the town fire-engine. Both transepts have aisles, a rare feature. Old glass, prints, portraits and books are to be found among memorials in stone and brass.

The grass vales around Melton contain many famous mansions, this in a county especially rich in gentlemen's seats. Brooksby Hall, overlooking the River Wreak, is a modernised Elizabethan manor house which was for many years the home of Admiral Beatty. Another Elizabethan mansion is Launde Abbey, which contains the remains of a priory of Black Canons. It is an E-shaped, two-storeyed building with gables and mullioned windows, and a fine little fifteenth-century chapel attached. Quenby Hall, whose long red-brick front and flat roof face the wooded summit of Billesden Coplow, is regarded as the finest Jacobean building in the county. It has been little altered in its three centuries of existence, retaining its diamond pattern brickwork and white stone quoins, and the six-sided tower rising above the porch. Its original iron gates stand in front of Leicester Museum. In the neighbourhood is Lowesby Hall, a fine red-brick Georgian house with a grand south-east front and entrance, possessing a large panelled hall with painted ceiling. Ingarsby, partly Gothic, and Baggrave, are two halls enclosed by prehistoric earthworks. Somerby, on its hill, was the home of Colonel Fred Burnaby, who achieved fame by his spectacular ride to Khiva last century.

The Wreak Valley separates the eastern wolds from the High

Wolds along the Nottinghamshire border. The valley was one of the highways by which the Danes penetrated the Midlands and the termination *by* to some sixty place-names shows how extensively they settled. The Wreak is a pleasant stream, from its junction with the Soar near Nine-Days-Wonder Bridge. Among old churches that at Gaddesby (105) has one of the four equestrian statues to be found in English parish churches. "Where they go to heaven on horseback," somebody described it to me, but the Colonel Cheney who had five horses shot under him at Waterloo escaped without a scratch. The monument is a huge thing, much too large for what is really a lovely little church built by the Knights Templars of Rothley some six or seven hundred years ago. Burton Lazars was the site of a twelfth-century lazar house, which was the chief leper hospital in England; it has a curious bell-turret of thirteenth-century workmanship.

North of the Wreak a triangular piece of Leicestershire thrusts eastward to Three Shires Bush, where Notts and Lincoln also meet. Here, among the heaving grasslands, are any number of sequestered upland villages, Prestwold, Wymeswold, Old Dalby and others, decayed market towns whose opulent-looking houses tell of former prosperity. Waltham-on-the-Wolds is such a place, with its church and windmill and old horse fair: Wymondham and Croxton Kerrial, with their fine stone-built houses, are others: the phrase "once a market town" epitomises their history. At Waltham, Redmile, Sibson and Grimston the curfew has been rung for twenty generations.

Many of these High Wold villages have lost their manor houses, but Goadby Marwood still has its double-fronted ironstone mansion, and Ragdale Old Hall (104) in brick and stone is one of the most picturesque houses in Leicestershire; it is now half farmhouse, half ruin. Four or five miles north of Melton is Ab-Kettleby, a pleasant village of thatch and gables grouped round the medieval church. I was told some yarns about a parson who formerly held the living there, but who resigned in order to become a racehorse trainer. He was so successful that he is said to have trained 119 winners. His last sermon was preached from the text, "So run that ye may obtain." During the First World War he managed a horseshoe factory, though I must confess that this was the first time I had heard of such an institution.

It was to Wartnaby, not far away, that Rider Haggard came to learn how Stilton cheeses were made, and was told "that except that they make less noise they are more troublesome than babies." *Rural England* was partly written here. This area might be suitably termed the windmill and Stilton cheese country. Little Dalby disputes with Wymondham the distinction of being the place where

106 BOTTESFORD CHURCH, LEICESTERSHIRE, WITH MONUMENTS OF
THE DE ROOS AND MANNERS FAMILIES

107   WOLLATON HALL, NOTTINGHAM.
ATTRIBUTED TO HUNTINGDON SMITHSON, *c.* 1580

108   IN CLIFTON VILLAGE, NOTTINGHAMSHIRE

this cheese was first made. It is called Stilton because it was first offered for sale by the owner of the Bell Inn, in Stilton, Hunts. A certain Mrs. Paulet, of Wymondham, or, according to the other story, a Mrs. Orton of Little Dalby, was the first person to make and sell the cheese to the innkeeper; afterwards its fame spread until now it is made in many parts of Leicestershire and Rutland. As for the windmills, you will see them scattered about on every hilltop; when I was there those at Harby and Saltby were still working, but Redmile's and Long Clawson's stood sailless and forlorn.

So we come to Belvoir Castle, the magnificent nineteenth-century towered and turreted mansion of the Duke of Rutland. Its battlemented walls and gatehouse crown a red sandstone escarpment above the wooded vale. "It is a strange sight to see how many steps of stairs the way goeth up from the village to the castel," says Leland, and that one sentence epitomises Belvoir; great mansions should be viewed from below to get the best effect. Belvoir has been called the most lordly place in England, Windsor Castle alone excepted, and seen from some distance away its fairy-palace effect stirs the imagination. Belvoir (pronounced Beever) is another place whose history goes back to that ubiquitous William who conquered England. He granted it to his standard-bearer Robert de Todeni, who built the first fortress. The castle was damaged in the Wars of the Roses, and practically destroyed after being besieged by the Roundheads. It was rebuilt when the monarchy was restored, and enlarged during the years 1800–16; later a disastrous fire compelled the rebuilding of the mansion on the present sumptuous lines. The result is a mixture of pseudo-Gothic, but some of the Norman walls remain, while the old Peacock Inn at the foot of the hill contains some slight remains of a priory founded by Todeni. Half the kings of England have visited Belvoir, and to attempt a list of the relics and art treasures which it contains would read like a sale catalogue.

The Vale of Belvoir is a rich pastoral district (17), with farms and pastures, noted for its barley and dairy produce. Here slate gives place to golden limestone, and lovely villages of mellow stonework stand on lush hillsides looking down upon the flat lands of Lincolnshire. The pride of the Vale is the church at Bottesford (106), the biggest village church in the county. It is mainly Early Perpendicular, with a lofty crocketed spire that is the highest in the county. It is a wonderful place for gargoyles and carvings, but it is the chancel and its memorials which attract the visitor, for here are some of the finest alabaster monuments in England. There are enough to grace a cathedral, the oldest being a diminutive figure in chain mail dating back to 1236. One fine tomb is that of Sir John Manners, father of the John Manners who carried off Dorothy Vernon from Haddon Hall. Curious stories are attached to two other memorials, one to two sons of the Manners family, "both of which died in their infancy by wicked Practice and Sorcerye," for which crime two maidservants at Belvoir were executed; the other is to the "fair maid of Normanton" who was killed by earwigs. The iron gates of the chancel are fine seventeenth-century craftsmanship. Bottesford also retains its old cross, stocks, whipping-post and seventeenth-century almshouse of brick whose inmates still wear the gowns prescribed by the Dr. Fleming who built the little bridge over the River Devon. Altogether, a rather fascinating little town.

The Wolds continue into Nottinghamshire, and there are so many other fascinating places that I can do no more than briefly outline the charms of a few. Bingham is an old-fashioned town that was once much larger than it is now. The church, once collegiate, has one of the finest broached spires in the county; note the portrait of Lily Langtry on the chancel screen. South of Bingham is Langar, which is the Battersby-on-the-Hill of *The Way of All Flesh*, for Samuel Butler was born in the red-brick rectory and wrote caustically of the local inhabitants. Its splendid cruciform church is known locally as the "Cathedral of the Vale." Here lie the Chaworths, from Wiverton Hall, one of whom was that Mary whom Byron loved in vain. The picturesque turreted gatehouse of the hall is the only original portion of the fortified manor garrisoned for Charles Stuart; the rest of the battlemented mansion is nineteenth-century.

Many of these villages on the Nottinghamshire Wolds have dwindled greatly in population during the last two centuries; the soil is stiff clay and difficult to work. It is a pleasant, restful country of windswept uplands and secluded woods with amber-coloured churches and forlorn windmills crowning the heights. Among edge-of-the-wold villages Widmerpol, Wysall, Stanton and Keyworth are typical of these dwindling settlements. As if marked out by a ruler the Fosse Way sweeps across the flat landscape to Newark, the straightest stretch of road in England. For over twenty miles it does not touch a single village; they all lie a mile or so away from the highway.

Much more interesting to follow is the river which flows past Clifton Grove to West Bridgford, that growing industrial outpost of Nottingham across the river. From Nottingham to Newark the river flows through pleasant pastoral country, now a wide meandering stream with meadows on either side, now flowing between high wooded banks with old villages perched aloft. Shelford is typical Notts scenery; pasture, ploughland and winding river. Shelford manor house and church figured in a dramatic action in the Civil War, for the place was stormed and captured and set on fire by the Roundheads, and Royalist snipers who had planted a cannon in the

109   THE EASTER SEPULCHRE   110   'THE PELICAN IN HER PIETY': THE SEDILIA

RICH DECORATED EXUBERANCE, HAWTON CHURCH, NOTTINGHAMSHIRE

111 THE INTERIOR, WYSOL CHURCH, NOTTINGHAMSHIRE

112 NEWARK, NOTTINGHAMSHIRE

church tower were burned out. In the village they will tell you a story of a local tailor who announced that he had fine crimson waistcoats for sale at moderate prices. They were such excellent value that people flocked to buy them, yet his stock of cloth never seemed to grow less. People wondered where he got the velvet from, and not until somebody remembered that he was also the sexton did they realise that he had been stripping the coffins of their funeral trappings!

Among the villages perched on the steep wooded river bank is Radcliffe-on-Trent, where a lovely memorial garden stands high above the river. East Bridgford has its old windmills and the site of the Roman fort of Margidunum. The brick Old Hall is little changed since the day when its owner, John Hacker, led King Charles to the scaffold. Past the Trent Hills the river flows to East Stoke where 7000 men died in the battle which finally brought to an end the Wars of the Roses. A steep track running down to the river is still called Red Gutter, and the name Deadman's Field tells its own story. It is a short walk to Elston, a pretty place among the trees, with an old black windmill that was grinding corn in 1938, and may still be doing so. The village was the home of the Darwins, Robert (who wrote the *Principia Botanica*) and Erasmus, the grand-father of the more famous Charles, though he himself was no mean physician, scientist, poet and inventor.

An old road leads down to the Trent ferry, where across the swiftly flowing stream is Bleasby, which claims to be the place where Paulinus baptised his converts when he made a missionary journey across the wilds of Nottinghamshire in the seventh century. A short distance away is Rolleston, the childhood home of Kate Greenaway. The many little villages tucked away in the wooded vales north of the Trent must be familiar to all Nottingham folk: Thurgarton with its old hall known as the Priory: Lowdham in its orchards and Lambley whose church walls are marked where archers sharpened their arrows. Oxton church is full of curious things. Laxton, further north, is the last place in England where the old open-field system of cultivation, general throughout the country in medieval times, is still practised.

Of several interesting villages between the Trent and the Vale of Belvoir there is only space to mention Hawton, two miles outside Newark. It has little but its church, but this is celebrated for its Easter Sepulchre (109). This was the recess in the wall where the figure of Christ was kept until Easter morning, before being carried in state to the High Altar. That at Hawton contains some of the most exquisite fourteenth-century stonework to be found in England (110). Carved figures show Roman soldiers, Christ rising from the tomb, and the Ascension scene; the arches and intricate decoration are a mass of feathery stonework.

Newark-on-Trent is a misnomer, for it stands some distance south of that stream, on the canalised River Devon. From across the river the town wears a most romantic appearance; its old bridge, castle, church spires and gabled houses lure you on (112). But I must confess to disappointment myself when I discovered that the magnificent walls and towers of the castle were just a shell, one-sided like a drop-scene in a theatre. Behind were only gardens and flower beds. Then I discovered all manner of old-fashioned things, coaching yards and archways and quaint alleys, which helped restore my belief in Newark's picturesque appeal. The Saxons called Newark the "Key of the North" when they rebuilt it after its destruction by the Northmen. Actually the castle is a brave-looking affair, the massive gatehouse and towers are all good Norman work, with graceful Perpendicular windows to mitigate their grimness. It was another of those "ruins that Cromwell knocked about a bit," for after standing three sieges during the Civil War his troops reduced it to its present picturesque appearance. All sorts of famous people came here, Queen Elizabeth, Cardinal Wolsey, kings and bishops; they still point out the room where King John died after being taken ill at Swineshead Abbey; beneath is a crypt and the dungeon where men were chained to the walls and left to die.

Newark is a famous place for old inns, for it was ever a town of comings and goings, from the days when the Romans marched along the Fosse Way to Lincoln and archers kept watch by the tower overlooking the Great North Road to these more prosaic times when people arrive and depart by the Flying Scot. The old inns with their cobbled courtyards, stables, outhouses and arched gateways retain the atmosphere of bygone centuries. Most of them are clustered about the market place, where is the stone to which bulls were fastened in the brave old days of bull-baiting. The Saracen's Head is one of the oldest inns, there having been an inn of that name since 1341. Charles I stayed there, and Sir Walter Scott, who often slept there, makes it Jeanie Deans' stopping-place in his *Heart of Midlothian*. The Clinton Arms next door was formerly the Kingston Arms, where Byron stayed while supervising the publication of his first book of poems. Here Gladstone made one of his first public speeches, and had the window in front of him shattered when a stone was hurled at his head. The culprit was released on promise of his vote the following day. Another old inn is the Ram, where George Eliot stayed while enjoying "some charming, quiet landscapes on the Trent"; but the Ossington Coffee Tavern, though built in the sixteenth-century style, is a modern erection. A draper's shop now occupies the White Hart Inn, one of the oldest domestic buildings in England. Its fourteenth-century front with overhanging storeys and gallery of painted figures is one of the most delightful things in Newark. Another fine black-and-white building is the picturesque Governor's House, three tiers of vaulted timber overhanging the street, where the governors of the castle lived during the Civil War. Other old timbered houses in Kirk Gate belonged to the twelfth-century St. Leonard's Hospital. The Magnus Grammar School is now a museum, restored to show the original Tudor schoolroom.

[Drawn by Hugh Mottram

THE QUEEN'S HEAD INN, NEWARK, NOTTINGHAMSHIRE

The Beaumond Cross is believed to be one of the Eleanor crosses erected by King Edward in 1290 to mark the funeral procession of his dead queen, from Harby to Charing Cross.

The parish church of St. Mary's (page 107) is the pride of the town. It is a fine cruciform building, originally Norman but now dating chiefly from the fifteenth century, with a lofty embattled western tower with pinnacles and octagonal spire which was completed just before the Black Death put an end to church-building for a time. The choir retains some fine stalls and screenwork, and is separated from the nave by a richly carved oak screen completed about 1508; the stone reredos is modern. On either side of the chancel are chantry chapels, the one on the south containing mural paintings depicting the Dance of Death. Among the few monuments which the church contains is a huge brass, nearly ten feet long, to Alan Fleming, who founded a chantry here in 1349; it is one of the largest in England. But brasses are not to everybody's taste, though there are several others, as well as some old glass, paintings, carvings, and part of the library left by a seventeenth-century vicar, though most of the rarities have been removed.

If you like prowling about old towns you will like Newark.

Beyond Newark the Trent meanders northward, through rich meadowlands broken by old water-courses, for the river has changed its bounds several times, and winding willow-lined streams mark its former channel. The pleasant village of Kelham faces the Trent where Newark ought to be. It was here, in an old house now superseded by the modern Theological College, that King Charles surrendered to the Scottish army. In the new chapel is Jaggers' masterpiece, a marvellous green bronze Crucifixion scene. Holme, on the eastern bank of the river, was on the western side until the Trent changed its course. The church has one of the few complete Tudor interiors. A room over the porch is known as Nan Scott's Chamber, after an old woman who took refuge there during the Great Plague. She brought with her enough food to last for several weeks, and remained in hiding there until all the rest of the inhabitants were dead. Almost every village along the Trent Valley seems to have something noteworthy about its church. It was at Harby, which is almost in Lincolnshire, that Edward I's gentle Queen Eleanor died, and when the funeral procession started out for Westminster Abbey, each resting-place on that solemn journey was marked by the erection of a stone cross, the last one of all being Charing Cross. Laneham church has a rare Norman door of weatherworn oak, and some thirteenth-century wooden seats roughly shaped by the adze. They are rare things to find nowadays. The Trent is tidal here, though many miles from the sea.

I have left till last Southwell, which must surely be one of the most surprising places in England. A small "city" of only 3000 people, it contains the least-known cathedral in England. It is a clean, tidy-looking place with red roofs gleaming among the greenery and any number of comfortable-looking houses. In fact, the town consists of five different parts, with open spaces in between, so that small though it is it occupies a considerable area. It is in

114 THE CHAPTER HOUSE ENTRANCE

113 DETAIL OF THE QUIRE SCREEN

THE RICHNESS OF DECORATED AT SOUTHWELL CATHEDRAL

115　EAST RETFORD CHURCH, FROM THE SOUTH-WEST

116　THE NORTH SIDE, SOUTHWELL CATHEDRAL,
NOTTINGHAMSHIRE

ROMANESQUE AND LATE GOTHIC

[Drawn by J. Johnson, F.S.A.

ST. MARY MAGDALEN CHURCH, NEWARK,
NOTTINGHAMSHIRE

High Town, or Southwell proper, that the square solid spires of the cathedral rise skyward from among the old prebendal houses and gardens along the River Greet. Beside the minster stands the Bishop's Palace, half fragmentary ruin, half modern villa, all that is left of the old medieval house to which the broken Wolsey came. Not far away is the old Saracen's Head Inn where another man spent his last hours of freedom; it is little changed since the day when Charles I stayed there before surrendering to the Scots at Kelham. Burgage Manor was the home of the Byrons, and when there was no money to maintain him at college the poet spent his time in Southwell's Assembly Room, performing in amateur theatricals and flirting with the girls, though he could write caustically enough concerning its inhabitants upon occasion.

It is obviously impossible within the space of a paragraph or two to give an adequate account of the cathedral; it deserves a book to itself. Tradition declares it to have been first established by Paulinus about 630, and for nearly 1000 years it was ruled by the powerful Archbishops of York. It became a collegiate church shortly after the Norman Conquest, to save the people of the district from having to make the annual arduous pilgrimage to York. During the Reformation it was more fortunate than neighbouring monastic establishments, and suffered little damage from the Roundheads. Fragmentary traces remain of the Saxon and early Norman churches, but broadly speaking the present structure is a fine example of a great Norman church of the middle of the twelfth century (116); it bears a striking resemblance, on a smaller scale, to York Minster. "Other churches may be older, a few may be larger, but none are more beautiful," is the verdict of a more competent authority than I. A Norman two-storeyed porch, a stately central tower and two high towers flanking the west entrances are, with the chapter house, the chief external features. The west front has been criticised because of its huge Perpendicular window which floods the Norman nave with light. The choir with its stone screen was called by Ruskin "the gem of English architecture," for elaborate and wonderful carvings make it a veritable picture-book. The chapter house is absolutely unrivalled, for "it is among chapter houses as the rose is among flowers" and contains the finest work ever accomplished in stone by English craftsmen (114).

The brass eagle on the lectern has a curious history, for formerly it belonged to Newstead Priory. When the monks were turned out of their home the prior filled the hollow ball on which the bird is standing with the parchment deeds of the monastery, in the hope that they could be recovered when the monks returned. The metal ball was cast into the lake for safety, but the monks never came back, and for nearly 300 years it lay buried under the water. When dug

[*Drawn by J. Johnson, F.S.A*

BINGHAM CHURCH, NOTTINGHAMSHIRE

NMC : P

up by accident it was sold as scrap metal to a Nottingham dealer. Later a prebend of Southwell bought it and presented it to the cathedral, when the lost documents were discovered inside.

Here are a couple of interesting titbits with which to finish the book. Over a hundred years ago a Mr. Bramley who lived just outside Southwell had an apple tree which had been raised from seed in a plant-pot. The tree produced such splendid fruit that cuttings were dispatched all over England. It became known as the "Bramley Seedling," and that is how your favourite cooking apple began its career. The old tree is still there.

And last of all: it was also over a hundred years ago that Byron's friend, the Rev. J. T. Becher, organised a plan by which local farm-workers, paying sixpence a week from the age of twenty, could secure sick pay and a pension of five shillings a week at the age of sixty-five. Shades of the post-war world in which we now find ourselves!

[*Drawn by Sydney R. Jones*

STONEY MIDDLETON, DERBYSHIRE

INDEX

The numerals in heavy type denote the figure numbers of the illustrations.

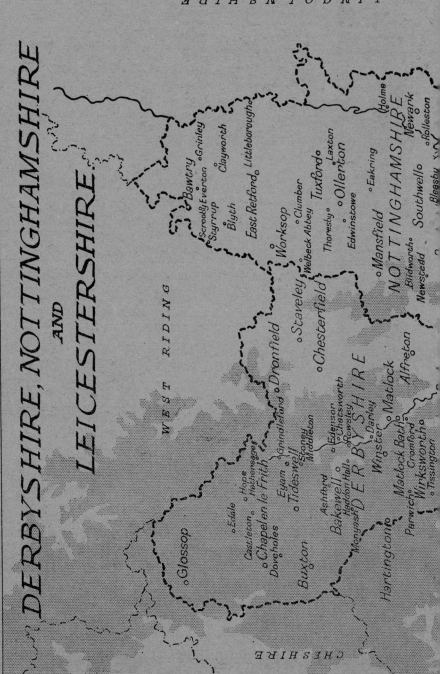

DERBYSHIRE, NOTTINGHAMSHIRE AND LEICESTERSHIRE.

LINCOLNSHIRE

WEST RIDING

LANCASHIRE

CHESHIRE

Glossop

Edale
Hope
Hathersage
Castleton
Chapel en le Frith
Doveholes
Eyam
Grindleford
Tideswell
Stoney Middleton
Edensor
Chatsworth
Rowsley
Ashford
Bakewell
Haddon Hall
Monyash
Buxton
Hartington
Parwich
Winster
Darley
Matlock
Matlock Bath
Cromford
Wirksworth
Tissington

DERBYSHIRE

Bawtry
Scrooby
Everton
Grinley
Styrrup
Blyth
Clayworth
East Retford
Littleborough
Worksop
Staveley
Dronfield
Chesterfield
Clumber
Welbeck Abbey
Thoresby
Tuxford
Laxton
Ollerton
Edwinstowe
Eakring
Mansfield
Holme
Newark
Rolleston
Southwell
Bleasby
Bidworth
Newstead

NOTTINGHAMSHIRE

Alfreton